TRAEGER GRILL RECIPE BOOK

The Complete Traeger Grill Cookbook With **80+** Mouth Satisfying Recipes.

Stephen Gilbert

TABLE OF CONTENTS

INTRODUCTION 7

BREAKFAST 9

1. Smoked Lamb Shoulder 9
2. Herby Lamb Chops 10
3. Garlic Rack of Lamb 12
4. Sweet & Spicy Chicken Thighs 14
5. Bacon Wrapped Chicken Breasts 15
6. Glazed Chicken Wings 17
7. Chicken Casserole 18
8. Buttered Turkey 19
9. Glazed Turkey Breast 21
10. Crispy Duck 22
11. Jerked Up Tilapia 23
12. Premium Salmon Nuggets 25
13. Creative Sablefish 27
14. Halibut Delight 29
15. Roast Rack of Lamb 30
16. Ultimate Lamb Burgers 31
17. Citrus- Smoked Trout 32

18. Sunday Supper Salmon with Olive Tapenade 34
19. Grilled Tuna 36
20. Grilled Swordfish 38

LUNCH 40

21. Lamb Kebabs 40
22. Grilled Carrots 41
23. Grilled Brussels Sprouts 42
24. Wood Pellet Spicy Brisket 43
25. Pellet Grill Funeral Potatoes 45
26. Smoky Caramelized Onions on the Pellet Grill 46
27. Hickory Smoked Green Beans 47
28. Smoked Corn on the Cob 49
29. Easy Grilled Corn 49
30. Seasoned Potatoes on Smoker 50
31. Atomic Buffalo Turds 51
32. Smashed Potato Casserole 53
33. Mushrooms Stuffed with Crab Meat 55
34. Bacon Wrapped with Asparagus 57
35. Bacon Cheddar Slider 58
36. Garlic Parmesan Wedge 60
37. Grilled Mushroom Skewers 62
38. Caprese Tomato Salad 65

39. Watermelon-Cucumber Salad 65

40. Fresh Creamed Corn 66

DINNER 68

41. Spinach Salad with Avocado and Orange 68

42. Raspberry and Blue Cheese Salad 69

43. Crunchy Zucchini Chips 70

44. Grilled Green Onions and Orzo and Sweet Peas 71

45. Tequila Slaw with Lime and Cilantro 72

46. Cranberry-Almond Broccoli Salad 73

47. Grilled French Dip 74

48. Roasted Cashews 75

49. Smoked Jerky 76

50. Bacon BBQ Bites 77

51. Smoked Guacamole 78

52. Jalapeno Poppers 79

53. Shrimp Cocktail 80

54. Deviled Eggs 81

55. Smoked Summer Sausage 82

56. Roasted Tomatoes 83

57. Onion Bacon Ring 84

58. Grilled Watermelon 85

59. Smoked Popcorn with Parmesan Herb 86

60. Breakfast Sausage 88

61. Corned Beef Hash 89

62. Turkey Sandwich 91

63. Scrambled Eggs 92

64. Berry Smoothie 93

APPETIZER AND SIDES 95

65. Avocado Smoothie 95

66. Tofu Smoothie 96

67. Banana Nut Oatmeal 97

68. Carrot Strawberry Smoothie 98

69. Green Smoothie 99

70. Kid-friendly Zucchini Bread 100

71. Breakfast Sausage Casserole 102

72. Keto Quiche 104

73. Smoked and Pulled Beef 106

74. Wood Pellet Smoked Beef Jerky 107

75. Reverse Seared Flank Steak 109

76. Smoked Midnight Brisket 110

77. Grilled Butter Basted Porterhouse Steak 112

78. Cocoa Crusted Grilled Flank steak 113

79. Wood Pellet Grill Prime Rib Roast 115

80. Smoked Longhorn Cowboy Tri-Tip 116

81. Wood Pellet Grill Teriyaki Beef Jerky 117

82. Grilled Butter Basted Rib-eye 118

83. Wood Pellet Smoked Brisket 119

84. Traeger Beef Jerky 121

85. Traeger Smoked Beef Roast 122

86. Reverse Seared Flank Steak 124

87. Traeger Beef Tenderloin 125

CONCLUSION 127

INTRODUCTION

Ever thought about grilling? Have you ever thought about owning your own grill that is easy to transport and allows for the convenience of grilling anywhere? These two guys did, which is why they created Traeger Grills. If you're looking for a grill that will make outdoor cooking easier than ever, then this might be the company for you! We'll be taking a closer look at their products and whether or not they're worth your time.

We'll also tell you some things to watch out for if you're considering buying one and how we tested these products ourselves.

So, what are those considerations you need to watch out for? What's the Best Size for A Traeger Grill?

The Traeger grill is either 18 inches by 24 inches or 22 inches by 22 inches, with an 8-and-a-half-inch height. We recommend the largest version as it has a slightly larger cooking surface and is taller, allowing you to fit more on your grill than you would otherwise.

This size is ideal for most families or if you have a barbecue party going on. If that's too big for you, then check out the smaller version that's also very useful and portable.

How Much Does a Traeger Grill Weigh?

Their first model is lightweight, as it only weighs in at 35 and a half pounds. It has a foldable stand that allows you to transport it easily, without taking up too much space. This grill is the most portable option on the market today and can be moved easily as it is so light weight.

This contributes to its overall attractiveness, making it one of those products that's just too good to pass up! You can easily take this grill wherever you want and use it for whatever occasion you need.

How Much Is a Traeger Grill?

A Traeger grill isn't cheap, but it's well worth the money. You're going to have to pay anywhere from $400 to $800 for a grill like this, depending on how many options you want.

One of the biggest considerations you'll have when purchasing a grill is how much it costs. This could be one of your biggest expenses, so you'll need to know if it's one that will pay off in the long run or not.

What Type of Cooking Surface Does the Traeger Have?

This grill is made with porcelain-coated steel grates that will withstand heat up to 500 degrees Fahrenheit without warping or deteriorating in any way. This keeps the food from falling through and makes it possible for you to cook anything you want.

The porcelain-coated steel is a ceramic material that heats up quickly and distributes heat evenly, making it an ideal choice for cooking meat or vegetables. If you took the time to find a new Traeger grill, then we say congratulations! You're going to be able to use it and begin cooking whatever you want in no time, without ever having to worry about how hot your fire is.

These grills are simple to use and take less than 5 minutes (sometimes) to set up. They can cook just about anything that you'd like without causing any damage or altering the flavor of the food in any way.

BREAKFAST

1. **Smoked Lamb Shoulder**

Preparation Time: 10 minutes

Cooking Time: 4 hours

Servings: 6

Ingredients:

- 8 pounds lamb shoulder, fat trimmed
- 2 tablespoons olive oil
- Salt as needed

For the Rub:

- 1 tablespoon dried oregano
- 2 tablespoons salt
- 1 tablespoon crushed dried bay leaf
- 1 tablespoon sugar
- 2 tablespoons dried crushed sage
- 1 tablespoon dried thyme
- 1 tablespoon ground black pepper
- 1 tablespoon dried basil
- 1 tablespoon dried rosemary
- 1 tablespoon dried parsley

Directions:

1. Switch on the Pellet grill, fill the grill hopper with cherry flavored wood pellets, power the grill on by using the control panel, select 'smoke' on the temperature dial, or set the temperature to 250 degrees F and let it preheat for a minimum of 5 minutes.
2. Meanwhile, prepare the rub and for this, take a small bowl, place all of its ingredients in it and stir until mixed.
3. Brush lamb with oil and then sprinkle with prepared rub until evenly coated.
4. When the grill has preheated, open the lid, place lamb should on the grill grate fat-side up, shut the grill and smoke for 3 hours.
5. Then change the smoking temperature to 325 degrees F and continue smoking to 1 hour until fat renders, and the internal temperature reaches 195 degrees F.
6. When done, wrap lamb should in aluminum foil and let it rest for 20 minutes.
7. Pull lamb shoulder by using two forks and then serve.

Nutrition: Calories: 300 Cal Fat: 24 g Carbs: 0 g Protein: 19 g Fiber: 0 g

2. Herby Lamb Chops

Preparation Time: 10 minutes

Cooking Time: 2 hours

Servings: 4

Ingredients:

- 8 lamb chops, each about ¾-inch thick, fat trimmed

For the Marinade:

- 1 teaspoon minced garlic
- Salt as needed
- 1 tablespoon dried rosemary
- Ground black pepper as needed
- ½ tablespoon dried thyme
- 3 tablespoons balsamic vinegar
- 1 tablespoon Dijon mustard
- ½ cup olive oil

Directions:

1. Prepare the marinade and for this, take a small bowl, place all of its ingredients in it and stir until well combined.
2. Place lamb chops in a large plastic bag, pour in marinade, seal the bag, turn it upside down to coat lamb chops with the marinade and let it marinate for a minimum of 4 hours in the refrigerator.
3. When ready to cook, switch on the Pellet grill, fill the grill hopper with flavored wood pellets, power the grill

on by using the control panel, select 'smoke' on the temperature dial, or set the temperature to 450 degrees F and let it preheat for a minimum of 5 minutes.

4. Meanwhile, remove lamb chops from the refrigerator and bring them to room temperature.
5. When the grill has preheated, open the lid, place lamb chops on the grill grate, shut the grill and smoke for 5 minutes per side until seared.
6. When done, transfer lamb chops to a dish, let them rest for 5 minutes and then serve.

Nutrition: Calories: 280 Cal Fat: 12.3 g Carbs: 8.3 g Protein: 32.7 g Fiber: 1.2 g

3. Garlic Rack of Lamb

Preparation Time: 10 minutes

Cooking Time: 3 hours

Servings: 4

Ingredients:

- 1 rack of lamb, membrane removed

For the Marinade:

- 2 teaspoons minced garlic
- 1 teaspoon dried basil
- 1/3 cup cream sherry
- 1 teaspoon dried oregano

- 1/3 cup Marsala wine
- 1 teaspoon dried rosemary
- ½ teaspoon ground black pepper
- 1/3 cup balsamic vinegar
- 2 tablespoons olive oil

Directions:

1. Prepare the marinade and for this, take a small bowl, place all of its ingredients in it and stir until well combined.
2. Place lamb rack in a large plastic bag, pour in marinade, seal the bag, turn it upside down to coat lamb with the marinade and let it marinate for a minimum of 45 minutes in the refrigerator.
3. When ready to cook, switch on the Pellet grill, fill the grill hopper with flavored wood pellets, power the grill on by using the control panel, select 'smoke' on the temperature dial, or set the temperature to 250 degrees F and let it preheat for a minimum of 5 minutes.
4. Meanwhile,
5. When the grill has preheated, open the lid, place lamb rack on the grill grate, shut the grill, and smoke for 3 hours until the internal temperature reaches 165 degrees F.

6. When done, transfer lamb rack to a cutting board, let it rest for 10 minutes, then cut into slices and serve.

Nutrition: Calories: 210 Cal Fat: 11 g Carbs: 3 g Protein: 25 g Fiber: 1 g

4. Sweet & Spicy Chicken Thighs

Preparation Time: 15 minutes

Cooking Time: 15 minutes

Servings: 4

Ingredients:

- 2 garlic cloves, minced
- ¼ cup honey
- 2 tablespoons soy sauce
- ¼ teaspoon red pepper flakes, crushed
- 4 (5-ounce) skinless, boneless chicken thighs
- 2 tablespoons olive oil
- 2 teaspoons sweet rub
- ¼ teaspoon red chili powder
- Ground black pepper, as required

Directions

1. Preheat the Z Grills Wood Pellet Grill & Smoker on grill setting to 400 degrees F.
2. In a small bowl, add garlic, honey, soy sauce and red pepper flakes and with a wire whisk, beat until well combined.

3. Coat chicken thighs with oil and season with sweet rub, chili powder and black pepper generously.
4. Arrange the chicken drumsticks onto the grill and cook for about 15 minutes per
5. In the last 4-5 minutes of cooking, coat drumsticks with garlic mixture.
6. Serve immediately.

Nutrition: Calories 309 Total Fat 12.1 g Saturated Fat 2.9 g Cholesterol 82 mg Sodium 504 mg Total Carbs 18.7 g Fiber 0.2 g Sugar 17.6 g Protein 32.3 g

5. Bacon Wrapped Chicken Breasts

Preparation Time: 0 minute

Cooking Time: 3 hours

Servings: 6

Ingredients:

For Brine:

- ¼ cup brown sugar
- ¼ cup kosher salt
- 4 cups water

   For Chicken:

- 6 skinless, boneless chicken breasts
- ¼ cup chicken rub
- 18 bacon slices
- 1½ cups BBQ sauce

Directions:

1. For brine: in a large pitcher, dissolve sugar and salt in water.
2. Place the chicken breasts in brine and refrigerate for about 2 hours, flipping once in the middle way.
3. Preheat the Z Grills Wood Pellet Grill & Smoker on grill setting to 230 degrees F.
4. Remove chicken breasts from brine and rinse under cold running water.
5. Season chicken breasts with rub generously.
6. Arrange 3 bacon strips of bacon onto a cutting board, against each other.
7. Place 1 chicken breast across the bacon, leaving enough bacon on the left side to wrap it over just a little.
8. Wrap the bacon strips around chicken breast and secure with toothpicks.
9. Repeat with remaining breasts and bacon slices.
10. Arrange the chicken breasts into pellet grill and cook for about 2½ hours.
11. Coat the breasts with BBQ sauce and cook for about 30 minutes more.
12. Serve immediately.

Nutrition: Calories 481 Total Fat 12.3 g Saturated Fat 4.2 g Cholesterol 41 mg Sodium 3000 mg Total Carbs 32 g Fiber 0.4g Sugar 22.2 g Protein 55.9 g

6. Glazed Chicken Wings

Preparation Time: 15 minutes

Cooking Time: 2 hours

Servings: 6

Ingredients:

- 2 pounds' chicken wings
- 2 garlic cloves, crushed
- 3 tablespoons hoisin sauce
- 2 tablespoons soy sauce
- 1 teaspoon dark sesame oil
- 1 tablespoon honey
- ½ teaspoon ginger powder
- 1 tablespoon sesame seeds, toasted lightly

Directions:

1. Preheat the Wood Pellet Grill & Smoker on grill setting to 225 degrees F.
2. Arrange the wings onto the lower rack of grill and cook for about 1½ hours.
3. Meanwhile, in a large bowl, mix together remaining all ingredients.
4. Remove wings from grill and place in the bowl of garlic mixture.
5. Coat wings with garlic mixture generously.
6. Now, set the grill to 375 degrees F.

7. Arrange the coated wings onto a foil-lined baking sheet and sprinkle with sesame seeds.
8. Place the pan onto the lower rack of pellet grill and cook for about 25-30 minutes.
9. Serve immediately.

Nutrition: Calories 336 Total Fat 13 g Saturated Fat 3.3 g Cholesterol 135 mg Sodium 560 mg Total Carbs 7.6 g Fiber 0.5 g Sugar 5.2 g Protein 44.7 g

7. **Chicken Casserole**

Preparation Time: 15 minutes

Cooking Time: 55 minutes

Servings: 8

Ingredients:

- 2 (15-ounce) cans cream of chicken soup
- 2 cups milk
- 2 tablespoons unsalted butter
- ¼ cup all-purpose flour
- 1 pound skinless, boneless chicken thighs, chopped
- ½ cup hatch chiles, chopped
- 2 medium onions, chopped
- 1 tablespoon fresh thyme, chopped
- Salt and ground black pepper, as required
- 1 cup cooked bacon, chopped
- 1 cup tater tots

Directions:

1. Preheat the Wood Pellet Grill & Smoker on grill setting to 400 degrees F.
2. In a large bowl, mix together chicken soup and milk.
3. In a skillet, melt butter over medium heat.
4. Slowly, add flour and cook for about 1-2 minutes or until smooth, stirring continuously.
5. Slowly, add soup mixture, beating continuously until smooth.
6. Cook until mixture starts to thicken, stirring continuously.
7. Stir in remaining ingredients except bacon and simmer for about 10-15 minutes.
8. Stir in bacon and transfer mixture into a 2½-quart casserole dish.
9. Place tater tots on top of casserole evenly.
10. Arrange the pan onto the grill and cook for about 30-35 minutes.
11. Serve hot.

Nutrition: Calories 440 Total Fat 25.8 g Saturated Fat 9.3 g Cholesterol 86 mg Sodium 1565 mg Total Carbs 22.2 g Fiber 1.5 g Sugar 4.6 g Protein 28.9 g

8. Buttered Turkey

Preparation Time: 15 minutes

Cooking Time: 4 hours

Servings: 16

Ingredients:

- ½ pound butter, softened
- 2 tablespoons fresh thyme, chopped
- 2 fresh rosemary, chopped
- 6 garlic cloves, crushed
- 1 (20-pound) whole turkey, neck and giblets removed
- Salt and ground black pepper, as required

Directions:

1. Preheat the Z Grills Wood Pellet Grill & Smoker on smoke setting to 300 degrees F, using charcoal.
2. In a bowl, place butter, fresh herbs, garlic, salt and black pepper and mix well.
3. With your fingers, separate the turkey skin from breast to create a pocket.
4. Stuff the breast pocket with ¼-inch thick layer of butter mixture.
5. Season the turkey with salt and black pepper evenly.
6. Arrange the turkey onto the grill and cook for 3-4 hours.
7. Remove turkey from pallet grill and place onto a cutting board for about 15-20 minutes before carving.
8. With a sharp knife, cut the turkey into desired-sized pieces and serve.

Nutrition: Calories 965 Total Fat 52 g Saturated Fat 19.9 g Cholesterol 385 mg Sodium 1916 mg Total Carbs 0.6 g Fiber 0.2 g Sugar 0 g Protein 106.5 g

9. Glazed Turkey Breast

Preparation Time: 15 minutes

Cooking Time: 4 hours

Servings: 6

Ingredients:

- ½ cup honey
- ¼ cup dry sherry
- 1 tablespoon butter
- 2 tablespoons fresh lemon juice
- Salt, as required
- 1 (3-3½-pound) skinless, boneless turkey breast

Directions:

1. In a small pan, place honey, sherry and butter over low heat and cook until the mixture becomes smooth, stirring continuously.
2. Remove from heat and stir in lemon juice and salt. Set aside to cool.
3. Transfer the honey mixture and turkey breast in a sealable bag.
4. Seal the bag and shake to coat well.
5. Refrigerate for about 6-10 hours.
6. Preheat the Wood Pellet Grill & Smoker on grill setting to 225-250 degrees F.

7. Place the turkey breast onto the grill and cook for about 2½-4 hours or until desired doneness.
8. Remove turkey breast from pallet grill and place onto a cutting board for about 15-20 minutes before slicing.
9. With a sharp knife, cut the turkey breast into desired-sized slices and serve.

Nutrition: Calories 443 Total Fat 11.4 g Saturated Fat 4.8 g Cholesterol 159 mg Sodium 138 mg Total Carbs 23.7 g Fiber 0.1 g Sugar 23.4 g Protein 59.2 g

10. Crispy Duck

Preparation Time: 15 minutes

Cooking Time: 4 hours 5 minutes

Servings: 6

Ingredients:

- ¾ cup honey
- ¾ cup soy sauce
- ¾ cup red wine
- 1 teaspoon paprika
- 1½ tablespoons garlic salt
- Ground black pepper, as required
- 1 (5-pound) whole duck, giblets removed and trimmed

Directions:

1. Preheat the Wood Pellet Grill & Smoker on grill setting to 225-250 degrees F.
2. In a bowl, add all ingredients except for duck and mix until well combined.
3. With a fork, poke holes in the skin of the duck.
4. Coat the duck with honey mixture generously.
5. Arrange duck in pellet gill, breast side down and cook for about 4 hours, coating with honey mixture one after 2 hours.
6. Remove the duck from grill and place onto a cutting board for about 15 minutes before carving.
7. With a sharp knife, cut the duck into desired-sized pieces and serve.

Nutrition: Calories 878 Total Fat 52.1 g Saturated Fat 13.9 g Cholesterol 3341 mg Sodium 2300 mg

Total Carbs 45.4 g Fiber 0.7 g Sugar 39.6 g Protein 51 g

11. Jerked Up Tilapia

Preparation Time: 20 minutes

Cooking Time: 45 minutes

Serving: 8

Ingredients:

- 5 cloves of garlic
- 1 small sized onion
- 3 Jalapeno Chiles

- 3 teaspoon of ground ginger
- 3 tablespoon of light brown sugar
- 3 teaspoon of dried thyme
- 2 teaspoons of salt
- 2 teaspoons of ground cinnamon
- 1 teaspoon of black pepper
- 1 teaspoon of ground allspice
- ¼ teaspoon of cayenne pepper
- 4 -6 ounce of tilapia fillets
- ¼ cup of olive oil
- 1 cup of sliced up carrots
- 1 bunch of whole green onions
- 2 tablespoon of whole allspice

Directions:

1. Take a blending bowl and combine the first 11 of the listed ingredients and puree them nicely using your blender or food processor
2. Add the fish pieces in a large-sized zip bag and toss in the pureed mixture alongside olive oil
3. Seal it up and press to make sure that the fish is coated well

4. Let it marinate in your fridge for at least 30 minutes to 1 hour
5. Take your drip pan and add water, cover with aluminum foil. Pre-heat your smoker to 225 degrees F
6. Use water fill water pan halfway through and place it over drip pan. Add wood chips to the side tray
7. Take a medium-sized bowl and toss in some pecan wood chips and soak them underwater alongside whole allspice
8. Prepare an excellent 9x 13-inch foil pan by poking a dozen holes and spraying it with non-stick cooking spray
9. Spread out the carrots, green onions across the bottom of the pan
10. Arrange the fishes on top of them
11. Place the container in your smoker
12. Smoke for about 45 minutes making sure to add more chips after every 15 minutes until the internal temperature of the fish rises to 145 degrees Fahrenheit
13. Serve hot

Nutrition: Calories: 347 Fats: 19g Carbs: 18g Fiber: 1g

12. **Premium Salmon Nuggets**

Preparation Time: 20 minutes +marinate time

Cooking Time: 1-2 hours

Servings: 8

Ingredients:

- 3 cups of packed brown sugar
- 1 cup of salt
- 1 tablespoon of onion, minced
- 2 teaspoons of chipotle seasoning
- 2 teaspoons of fresh ground black pepper
- 1 garlic clove, minced
- 1-2 pound of salmon fillets, cut up into bite-sized portions

Directions:

1. Take a large-sized bowl and stir in brown sugar, salt, chipotle seasoning, onion, garlic and pepper
2. Transfer salmon to a large shallow marinating dish
3. Pour dry marinade over fish and cover, refrigerate overnight
4. Take your drip pan and add water, cover with aluminum foil. Pre-heat your smoker to 180 degrees F
5. Use water fill water pan halfway through and place it over drip pan. Add wood chips to the side tray
6. Rinse the salmon chunks thoroughly and remove salt
7. Transfer them to grill rack and smoke for 1-2 hours

8. Remove the heat and enjoy it!

Nutrition: Calories: 120 Fats: 18g Carbs: 3g Fiber: 2g

13. Creative Sablefish

Preparation Time: 15 minutes

Cooking Time: 3 hours

Servings: 8

Ingredients:

- 2-3 pounds of sablefish fillets
- 1 cup of kosher salts
- ¼ cup of sugar
- 2 tablespoon of garlic powder
- Honey for glazing
- Sweet paprika for dusting

Directions:

1. Take a bowl and mix salt, garlic powder, and sugar
2. Pour on a healthy layer of your mix into a lidded plastic tub, large enough to hold the fish
3. Cut up the fillet into pieces
4. Gently massage the salt mix into your fish meat and place them with the skin side down on to the salt mix in the plastic tub

5. Cover up the container and keep it in your fridge for as many hours as the fish weighs
6. Remove the sablefish from the tub and place it under cold water for a while
7. Pat, it dries using a kitchen towel and puts it back to the fridge, keep it uncovered overnight
8. Take your drip pan and add water, cover with aluminum foil. Pre-heat your smoker to 225 degrees F
9. Use water fill water pan halfway through and place it over drip pan. Add wood chips to the side tray
10. Smoke for 2-3 hours
11. After the first hour of smoking, make sure to baste the fish with honey and keep repeating this after every hour
12. One done, move the fish to a cooling rack and baste it with honey one last time
13. Let it cool for about an hour
14. Use tweezers to pull out the bone pins
15. Dust the top with some paprika and wait for 30 minutes to let the paprika sink in
16. Put the fish in your fridge
17. Serve hot or chilled!

Nutrition: Calories: 171 Fats: 10g Carbs: 13g Fiber: 1g

14. **Halibut Delight**

Preparation Time: 4-6 hours

Cooking Time: 15 minutes

Servings: 4-6

Ingredients:

- ½ a cup of salt
- ½ a cup of brown sugar
- 1 teaspoon of smoked paprika
- 1 teaspoon of ground cumin
- 2 pound of halibut
- 1/3 cup of mayonnaise

Directions:

1. Take a small bowl and add salt, brown sugar, cumin, and paprika
2. Coat the halibut well and cover, refrigerate for 4-6 hours
3. Take your drip pan and add water, cover with aluminum foil. Pre-heat your smoker to 200 degrees F
4. Use water fill water pan halfway through and place it over drip pan. Add wood chips to the side tray
5. Remove the fish from refrigerator and rinse it well, pat it dry
6. Rub the mayonnaise on the fish

7. Transfer the halibut to smoker and smoke for 2 hours until the internal temperature reaches 120 degrees Fahrenheit

Nutrition: Calories: 375 Fats: 21g Carbs: 10g Fiber: 2g

15. Roast Rack of Lamb

Preparation Time: 10 minutes

Cooking Time: 1 hour

Servings: 6-8

Ingredients:

- Wood Pellet Flavor: Alder
- 1 (2-pound) rack of lamb
- 1 batch Rosemary-Garlic Lamb Seasoning

Directions:

1. Supply your smoker with wood pellets and follow the manufacturer's specific start-up procedure. Preheat the grill to 450°F.
2. Using a boning knife, score the bottom fat portion of the rib meat.
3. Using your hands, rub the rack of lamb with the lamb seasoning, making sure it penetrates into the scored fat.
4. Place the rack directly on the grill grate and smoke until its internal temperature reaches 145F.

5. Take off the rack from the grill and let it rest for 20 to 30 minutes, before slicing into individual ribs to serve.

Nutrition: Calories: 50 Carbs: 4g Fiber: 2g Fat: 2.5g Protein: 2g

16. Ultimate Lamb Burgers

Preparation Time: 20 minutes

Cooking Time: 30 minutes

Servings: 4

Ingredients:

Pellets: Apple

Burger:

- 2 lbs. ground lamb
- 1 jalapeño
- 6 scallions, diced
- 2 tablespoons mint
- 2 tablespoons dill, minced
- 3 cloves garlic, minced
- Salt and pepper
- 4 brioche buns
- 4 slices manchego cheese

Sauce:

- 1 cup mayonnaise
- 2 teaspoons lemon juice
- 2 cloves garlic
- 1 bell pepper, diced

- salt and pepper

Directions

1. When ready to cook, turn your smoker to 400F and preheat.
2. Add the mint, scallions, salt, garlic, dill, jalapeño, lamb, and pepper to the mixing bowl.
3. Form the lamb mixture into eight patties.
4. Lay the pepper on the grill and cook for 20 minutes.
5. Take the pepper from the grill and place it in a bag, and seal. After ten minutes, remove pepper from the bag, remove seeds and peel the skin.
6. Add the garlic, lemon juice, mayo, roasted red pepper, salt, and pepper and process until smooth. Serve alongside the burger.
7. Lay the lamb burgers on the grill, and cook for five minutes per side, then place in the buns with a slice of cheese, and serve with the homemade sauce.

Nutrition: Calories: 50 Carbs: 4g Fiber: 2g Fat: 2.5g Protein: 2g

17. **Citrus- Smoked Trout**

Preparation Time: 10 minutes

Cooking Time: 1 to 2 hours

Servings: 6 to 8

Ingredients:

- 6 to 8 skin-on rainbow trout, cleaned and scaled
- 1-gallon orange juice
- ½ cup packed light brown sugar
- ¼ cup salt
- 1 tablespoon freshly ground black pepper
- Nonstick spray, oil, or butter, for greasing
- 1 tablespoon chopped fresh parsley
- 1 lemon, sliced

Directions:

1. Fillet the fish and pat dry with paper towels
2. Pour the orange juice into a large container with a lid and stir in the brown sugar, salt, and pepper
3. Place the trout in the brine, cover, and refrigerate for 1 hour
4. Cover the grill grate with heavy-duty aluminum foil. Poke holes in the foil and spray with cooking spray
5. Supply your smoker with wood pellets and follow the manufacturer's specific start-up procedure. Preheat, with the lid closed, to 225°F
6. Remove the trout from the brine and pat dry. Arrange the fish on the foil-covered grill grate, close the lid, and smoke for 1 hour 30 minutes to 2 hours, or until flaky

7. Remove the fish from the heat. Serve garnished with the fresh parsley and lemon slices.

Nutrition: Calories: 220, Protein: 33 g Fat: 4 g, Carbohydrates: 17 g,

18. Sunday Supper Salmon with Olive Tapenade

Preparation Time: 1 hour and 20 minutes

Cooking Time: 1 to 2 hours

Servings: 10 to 12

Ingredients:

- 2 cups packed light brown sugar
- ½ cup salt
- ¼ cup maple syrup
- ⅓ cup crab boil seasoning
- 1 (3- to 5-pound) whole salmon fillet, skin removed
- ¼ cup extra-virgin olive oil
- 1 (15-ounce) can pitted green olives, drained
- 1 (15-ounce) can pitted black olives, drained
- 3 tablespoons jarred sun-dried tomatoes, drained
- 3 tablespoons chopped fresh basil
- 1 tablespoon dried oregano
- 2 tablespoons freshly squeezed lemon juice
- 2 tablespoons jarred capers, drained
- 2 tablespoons chopped fresh parsley, plus more for sprinkling

Directions:

1. In a medium bowl, combine the brown sugar, salt, maple syrup, and crab boil seasoning.
2. Rub the paste all over the salmon and place the fish in a shallow dish. Cover and marinate in the refrigerator for at least 8 hours or overnight.
3. Remove the salmon from dish, rinse, and pat dry, and let stand for 1 hour to take off the chill.
4. Meanwhile, in a food processor, pulse the olive oil, green olives, black olives, sun-dried tomatoes, basil, oregano, lemon juice, capers, and parsley to a chunky consistency. Refrigerate the tapenade until ready to serve.
5. Supply your smoker with wood pellets and follow the manufacturer's specific start-up procedure. Preheat, with the lid closed, to 250°F.
6. Place the salmon on the grill grate (or on a cedar plank on the grill grate), close the lid, and smoke for 1 to 2 hours, or until the internal temperature reaches 140°F to 145°F. When the fish flakes easily with a fork, it's done.
7. Remove the salmon from the heat and sprinkle with parsley. Serve with the olive tapenade.

Nutrition: Calories: 240; Proteins: 23g; Carbs: 3g; Fat: 16g

19. **Grilled Tuna**

Preparation Time: 20 minutes

Cooking Time: 4 hours

Servings: 6

Ingredients:

- Albacore tuna fillets – 6, each about 8 ounces
- Salt – 1 cup
- Brown sugar – 1 cup
- Orange, zested – 1
- Lemon, zested – 1

Directions:

1. Before preheating the grill, brine the tuna, and for this, prepare brine stirring together all of its ingredients until mixed.
2. Take a large container, layer tuna fillets in it, covering each fillet with it, and then let them sit in the refrigerator for 6 hours.
3. Then remove tuna fillets from the brine, rinse well, pat dry and cool in the refrigerator for 30 minutes.
4. When the grill has preheated, place tuna fillets on the grilling rack and let smoke for 3 hours, turning halfway.
5. Check the fire after one hour of smoking and add more wood pallets if required.
6. Then switch temperature of the grill to 225 degrees F and continue grilling for another 1 hour until tuna has turned nicely golden and fork-tender.
7. Serve immediately.

Nutrition: Calories: 311; Fiber: 3 g; Saturated Fat: 1.2 g; Protein: 45 g; Carbs: 11 g; Total Fat: 8.8 g; Sugar: 1.3 g

20. **Grilled Swordfish**

Preparation Time: 10 minutes

Cooking Time: 18 minutes

Servings: 4

Ingredients:

- Swordfish fillets – 4
- Salt – 1 tablespoon
- Ground black pepper – ¾ tablespoon
- Olive oil – 2 tablespoons
- Ears of corn – 4
- Cherry tomatoes – 1 pint
- Cilantro, chopped – 1/3 cup

- Medium red onion, peeled, diced – 1
- Serrano pepper, minced – 1
- Lime, juiced – 1
- Salt – ½ teaspoon
- Ground black pepper – ¼ teaspoon

Directions:

1. In the meantime, prepare fillets and for this, brush them with oil and then season with salt and black pepper.
2. Prepare the corn, and for this, brush with olive oil and season with ¼ teaspoon each of salt and black pepper.
3. When the grill has preheated, place fillets on the grilling rack along with corns and grill corn for 15 minutes until light brown and fillets for 18 minutes until fork tender.
4. When corn has grilled, cut kernels from it, place them into a medium bowl, add remaining ingredients for the salsa and stir until mixed.
5. When fillets have grilled, divide them evenly among plates, top with corn salsa and then serve.

Nutrition: Calories: 311; Total Fat: 8.8 g; Saturated Fat: 1.2 g; Fiber: 3 g; Protein: 45 g; Sugar: 1.3 g Carbs: 11 g;

LUNCH

21. Lamb Kebabs

Preparation Time: 15 minutes

Cooking Time: 10 minutes

Servings: 4

Ingredients:

Pellets: Mesquite

- 1/2 tablespoon salt
- 2 tablespoons fresh mint
- 3 lbs. leg of lamb
- 1/2 cup lemon juice
- 1 tablespoon lemon zest
- 15 apricots, pitted
- 1/2 tablespoon cilantro
- 2 teaspoons black pepper
- 1/2 cup olive oil
- 1 teaspoon cumin
- 2 red onion

Directions:

1. Combine the olive oil, pepper, lemon juice, mint, salt, lemon zest, cumin, and cilantro. Add lamb leg, then place in the refrigerator overnight.

2. Remove the lamb from the marinade, cube them, and then thread onto the skewer with the apricots and onions.
3. When ready to cook, turn your smoker to 400F and preheat.
4. Lay the skewers on the grill and cook for ten minutes.
5. Remove from the grill and serve.

Nutrition: Calories: 50 Carbs: 4g Fiber: 2g Fat: 2.5g Protein: 2g

22. **Grilled Carrots**

Preparation Time: 5 Minutes

Cooking Time: 20 Minutes

Servings: 6

Ingredients

- 1 lb. carrots, large
- 1/2 tbsp. salt
- 6 oz. butter
- 1/2 tbsp. black pepper
- Fresh thyme

Direction

1. Thoroughly wash the carrots and do not peel. Pat them dry and coat with olive oil.
2. Add salt to your carrots.
3. Meanwhile, preheat a pellet grill to 350°F.

4. Now place your carrots directly on the grill or on a raised rack.

5. Close and cook for about 20 minutes.

6. While carrots cook, cook butter in a saucepan, small, over medium heat until browned. Stir constantly to avoid it from burning. Remove from heat.

7. Remove carrots from the grill onto a plate then drizzle with browned butter.

8. Add pepper and splash with thyme.

9. Serve and enjoy.

Nutrition: Calories 250, Total fat 25g, Saturated fat 15g, Total Carbs 6g, Net Carbs 4g, Protein 1g, Sugars 3g, Fiber 2g, Sodium 402mg, Potassium 369mg

23. Grilled Brussels Sprouts

Preparation Time: 15 Minutes

Cooking Time: 20 Minutes

Servings: 8

Ingredients

- 1/2 lb. bacon, grease reserved
- 1 lb. Brussels Sprouts
- 1/2 tbsp. pepper
- 1/2 tbsp. salt

Directions:

1. Cook bacon until crispy on a stovetop, reserve its grease then chop into small pieces.
2. Meanwhile, wash the Brussels sprouts, trim off the dry end, and remove dried leaves if any. Half them and set aside.
3. Place 1/4 cup reserved grease in a pan, cast-iron, over medium-high heat.
4. Season the Brussels sprouts with pepper and salt.
5. Brown the sprouts on the pan with the cut side down for about 3-4 minutes.
6. In the meantime, preheat your pellet grill to 350-375ºF.
7. Place bacon pieces and browned sprouts into your grill-safe pan.
8. Cook for about 20 minutes.
9. Serve immediately.

Nutrition: Calories 153, Total fat 10g, Saturated fat 3g, Total Carbs 5g, Net Carbs 3g, Protein 11g, Sugars 1g, Fiber 2g, Sodium 622mg, Potassium 497mg

24. Wood Pellet Spicy Brisket

Preparation Time: 20 Minutes

Cooking Time: 9 Hours

Servings: 10

Ingredients
- 2 tbsp. garlic powder
- 2 tbsp. onion powder
- 2 tbsp. paprika
- 2 tbsp. chili powder
- 1/3 cup salt
- 1/3 cup black pepper
- 12 lb. whole packer brisket, trimmed
- 1-1/2 cup beef broth

Directions:
1. Set your wood pellet temperature to 225°F. Let preheat for 15 minutes with the lid closed.
2. Meanwhile, mix garlic, onion, paprika, chili, salt, and pepper in a mixing bowl.
3. The brisket generously on all sides.
4. Place the meat on the grill with the fat side down and let it cool until the internal temperature reaches 160°F.
5. Remove the meat from the grill and double wrap it with foil. Return it to the grill and cook until the internal temperature reaches 204°F.

6. Remove from grill, unwrap the brisket and let rest for 15 minutes.
7. Slice and serve.

Nutrition: Calories 270, Total fat 20g, Saturated fat 8g, Total Carbs 3g, Net Carbs 3g, Protein 20g, Sugar 1g, Fiber 0g, Sodium: 1220mg

25. **Pellet Grill Funeral Potatoes**

Preparation Time: 10 Minutes

Cooking Time: 60 Minutes

Servings: 8

Ingredients

- 1, 32 oz., package frozen hash browns
- 1/2 cup cheddar cheese, grated
- 1 can cream of chicken soup
- 1 cup sour cream
- 1 cup Mayonnaise
- 3 cups corn flakes, whole or crushed
- 1/4 cup melted butter

Directions:

1. Preheat your pellet grill to 350°F.
2. Spray a 13 x 9 baking pan, aluminum, using a cooking spray, non-stick.

3. Mix hash browns, cheddar cheese, chicken soup cream, sour cream, and mayonnaise in a bowl, large.
4. Spoon the mixture into a baking pan gently.
5. Mix corn flakes and melted butter then sprinkle over the casserole.
6. Grill for about 1-1/2 hours until potatoes become tender. If the top browns too much, cover using a foil until potatoes are done.
7. Remove from the grill and serve hot.

Nutrition: Calories 403, Total fat 37g, Saturated fat 12g, Total Carbs 14g, Net Carbs 14g, Protein 4g, Sugars 2g, Fiber 0g, Sodium 620mg, Potassium 501mg

26. Smoky Caramelized Onions on the Pellet Grill

Preparation Time: 5 Minutes

Cooking Time: 60 Minutes

Servings: 4

Ingredients

- 5 large, sliced onions
- 1/2 cup fat of your choice
- Pinch of Sea salt

Directions:

1. Place all the ingredients into a pan. For a deep rich brown caramelized onion, cook them off for about 1hour on a stovetop.
2. Keep the grill temperatures not higher than 250 - 275°F.
3. Now transfer the pan into the grill.
4. Cook for about 1-1½ hours until brown in color. Check and stir with a spoon, wooden, after every 15 minutes. Make sure not to run out of pellets.
5. Now remove from the grill and season with more salt if necessary.
6. Serve immediately or place in a refrigerator for up to 1 week.

Nutrition: Calories 286, Total fat 25.8g, Saturated fat 10.3g, Total Carbs 12.8g, Net Carbs 9.8g, Protein 1.5g, Sugars 5.8g, Fiber 3g Sodium 6mg, Potassium 201mg

27. Hickory Smoked Green Beans

Preparation Time: 15 Minutes

Cooking Time: 3 Hours

Servings: 10

Ingredients

- 6 cups fresh green beans, halved and ends cut off
- 2 cups chicken broth
- 1 tbsp. pepper, ground

- 1/4 tbsp. salt
- 2 tbsp. apple cider vinegar
- 1/4 cup diced onion
- 6-8 bite-size bacon slices
- **Optional:** sliced almonds

Directions:
1. Add green beans to a colander then rinse well. Set aside.
2. Place chicken broth, pepper, salt, and apple cider in a pan, large. Add green beans.
3. Blanch over medium heat for about 3-4 minutes then remove from heat.
4. Transfer the mixture into an aluminum pan, disposable. Make sure all mixture goes into the pan so do not drain them.
5. Place bacon slices over the beans and place the pan into the wood pellet smoker,
6. Smoke for about 3 hours uncovered.
7. Remove from the smoker and top with almonds slices.
8. Serve immediately.

Nutrition: Calories 57, Total fat 3g, Saturated fat 1g, Total Carbs 6g, Net Carbs 4g, Protein 4g, Sugars 2g, Fiber 2g, Sodium 484mg, Potassium 216mg

28. Smoked Corn on the Cob

Preparation Time: 5 Minutes

Cooking Time: 60 Minutes

Servings: 4

Ingredients

- 4 corn ears, husk removed
- 4 tbsp. olive oil
- Pepper and salt to taste

Directions:

1. Preheat your smoker to 225°F.
2. Meanwhile, brush your corn with olive oil. Season with pepper and salt.
3. Place the corn on a smoker and smoke for about 1 hour 15 minutes.
4. Remove from the smoker and serve.
5. Enjoy!

Nutrition: Calories 180, Total fat 7g, Saturated fat 4g, Total Carbs 31g, Net Carbs 27g, protein 5g, Sugars 5g, Fiber 4g, Sodium 23mg, Potassium 416mg

29. Easy Grilled Corn

Preparation Time: 5 Minutes

Cooking Time: 40 Minutes

Servings: 6

Ingredients

- 6 fresh corn ears, still in the husk
- Pepper, salt, and butter

Directions:

1. Preheat your wood pellet grill to 375-400°F.
2. Cut off the large silk ball from the corn top and any hanging or loose husk pieces.
3. Place the corn on your grill grate directly and do not peel off the husk.
4. Grill for about 30-40 minutes. Flip a few times to grill evenly all round.
5. Transfer the corn on a platter, serve, and let guests peel their own.
6. Now top with pepper, salt, and butter.
7. Enjoy!

Nutrition: Calories 77, Total fat 1g, Saturated fat 1g, Total carbs 17g, Net carbs 15g, Protein 3g, Sugars 6g, Fiber 2g, Sodium 14mg, Potassium 243mg

30. **Seasoned Potatoes on Smoker**

Preparation Time: 10 Minutes

Cooking Time: 45 Minutes

Servings: 6

Ingredients

- 1-1/2 lb. creamer potatoes
- 2 tbsp. olive oil
- 1 tbsp. garlic powder
- 1/4 tbsp. oregano
- 1/2 tbsp. thyme, dried
- 1/2 tbsp. parsley, dried

Directions:

1. Preheat your pellet grill to 350°F.
2. Spray an 8x8 inch foil pan using non-stick spray.
3. Mix all ingredients in the pan and place it into the grill.
4. Cook for about 45 minutes until potatoes are done. Stir after every 15 minutes.
5. Serve and enjoy!

Nutrition: Calories 130, Total fat 4g, Saturated fat 2g, Total Carbs 20g, Net Carbs 18g, Protein 2g, Sugars 2g, Fiber 2g, Sodium 7mg, Potassium 483mg

31. Atomic Buffalo Turds

Preparation Time: 30-45 minutes

Cooking Time: 1.5 hours to 2 hours

Servings: 6-10

Recommended pellets: Hickory, blend

Ingredients:
- 10 Medium Jalapeno Pepper
- 8 oz. regular cream cheese at room temperature
- ¾ Cup Monterey Jack and Cheddar Cheese Blend Shred (optional)
- 1 teaspoon smoked paprika
- 1 tsp garlic powder
- 1/2 teaspoon cayenne pepper
- Teaspoon red pepper flakes (optional)
- 20 smoky sausages
- 10 sliced bacon, cut in half

Directions:
1. Wear food service gloves when using. Jalapeno peppers are washed vertically and sliced. Carefully remove seeds and veins using a spoon or paring knife and discard. Place Jalapeno on a grilled vegetable tray and set aside.
2. In a small bowl, mix cream cheese, shredded cheese, paprika, garlic powder, cayenne pepper if used, and red pepper flakes if used, until thoroughly mixed.
3. Mix cream cheese with half of the jalapeno pepper.
4. Place the Little Smokies sausage on half of the filled jalapeno pepper.

5. Wrap half of the thin bacon around half of each jalapeno pepper.
6. Fix the bacon to the sausage with a toothpick so that the pepper does not pierce. Place the ABT on the grill tray or pan.
7. Set the wood pellet smoker grill for indirect cooking and preheat to 250 degrees Fahrenheit using hickory pellets or blends.
8. Suck jalapeno peppers at 250 ° F for about 1.5 to 2 hours until the bacon is cooked and crisp.
9. Remove the ABT from the grill and let it rest for 5 minutes before hors d'oeuvres.

32. **Smashed Potato Casserole**

Preparation Time: 30-45 minutes

Cooking Time: 45-60 minutes

Servings: 8

Recommended pellet: Optional

Ingredients:

- 8-10 bacon slices
- ¼ cup (½ stick) salt butter or bacon grease
- 1 sliced red onion
- 1 sliced small pepper
- 1 sliced small red pepper

- 1 sliced small pepper
- 3 cups mashed potatoes
- ¾ cup sour cream
- 1.5 teaspoon Texas BBQ Love
- 3 cups of sharp cheddar cheese
- 4 cups hashed brown potato

Directions:

1. Cook the bacon in a large skillet over medium heat until both sides are crispy for about 5 minutes. Set the bacon aside.
2. Transfer the rendered bacon grease to a glass container.
3. In the same large frying pan, heat the butter or bacon grease over medium heat and fry the red onions and peppers until they become al dente. Set aside.
4. Spray a 9 x 11-inch casserole dish with a non-stick cooking spray and spread the mashed potatoes to the bottom of the dish.
5. Layer sour cream on mashed potatoes and season with Texas BBQ Love.
6. Layer the stir-fried vegetables on the potatoes and pour butter or bacon grease into a pan.
7. Sprinkle 1.5 cups of sharp cheddar cheese followed by frozen hash brown potatoes.

8. Spoon the remaining butter or bacon grease from the stir-fried vegetables over the hash browns and place the crushed bacon.

9. Place the remaining 1.5 cups of sharp cheddar cheese and cover the casserole dish with a lid or aluminum foil.

10. Using the selected pellets, set up a wood pellet smoking grill for indirect cooking and preheat to 350 ° F.

11. Bake the crushed potato casserole for 45-60 minutes until the cheese foams.

12. Rest for 10 minutes before eating.

33. **Mushrooms Stuffed with Crab Meat**

Preparation Time: 20 minutes

Cooking Time: 30-45 minutes

Servings: 4-6

Recommended pellet: Optional

Ingredients:

- 6 medium-sized portobello mushrooms
- Extra virgin olive oil
- 1/3 Grated parmesan cheese cup
- Club Beat Staffing:
- 8 oz. fresh crab meat or canned or imitation crab meat
- 2 tablespoons extra virgin olive oil

- 1/3 Chopped celery
- Chopped red peppers
- ½ cup chopped green onion
- ½ cup Italian breadcrumbs
- ½Cup mayonnaise
- 8 oz. cream cheese at room temperature
- 1/2 teaspoon of garlic
- 1 tablespoon dried parsley
- Grated parmesan cheese cup
- 1 1 teaspoon of Old Bay seasoning
- ¼ teaspoon of kosher salt
- ¼ teaspoon black pepper

Directions:

1. Clean the mushroom cap with a damp paper towel. Cut off the stem and save it.
2. Remove the brown gills from the bottom of the mushroom cap with a spoon and discard.
3. Prepare crab meat stuffing. If you are using canned crab meat, drain, rinse, and remove shellfish.
4. Heat the olive oil in a frying pan over medium high heat. Add celery, peppers and green onions and fry for 5 minutes. Set aside for cooling.

5. Gently pour the chilled sauteed vegetables and the remaining ingredients into a large bowl.
6. Cover and refrigerate crab meat stuffing until ready to use.
7. Put the crab mixture in each mushroom cap and make a mound in the center.
8. Sprinkle extra virgin olive oil and sprinkle parmesan cheese on each stuffed mushroom cap. Put the mushrooms in a 10 x 15-inch baking dish.
9. Use the pellets to set the wood pellet smoker grill to indirect heating and preheat to 375 ° F.
10. Bake for 30-45 minutes until the filling becomes hot (165 degrees Fahrenheit as measured by an instant-read digital thermometer) and the mushrooms begin to release juice.

34. **Bacon Wrapped with Asparagus**

Preparation Time: 15 minutes

Cooking Time: 25-30 minutes

Servings: 4-6

Recommended pellet: Optional

- 1-pound fresh thick asparagus (15-20 spears)
- Extra virgin olive oil
- 5 sliced bacon

- 1 teaspoon of Western Love or salted pepper

Directions:

1. Cut off the wooden ends of the asparagus and make them all the same length.
2. Divide the asparagus into a bundle of three spears and split with olive oil. Wrap each bundle with a piece of bacon, then dust with seasonings or salt pepper for seasoning.
3. Set the wood pellet smoker grill for indirect cooking and place a Teflon coated fiberglass mat on the grate (to prevent asparagus from sticking to the grate grate). Preheat to 400 degrees Fahrenheit using all types of pellets. The grill can be preheated during asparagus Preparation Guide.
4. Bake the asparagus wrapped in bacon for 25-30 minutes until the asparagus is soft and the bacon is cooked and crispy.

35. **Bacon Cheddar Slider**

Preparation Time: 30 minutes

Cooking Time: 15 minutes

Servings: 6-10 (1-2 sliders each as an appetizer)

Recommended pellet: Optional

Ingredients:

- 1-pound ground beef (80% lean)

- 1/2 teaspoon of garlic salt
- 1/2 teaspoon salt
- 1/2 teaspoon of garlic
- 1/2 teaspoon onion
- 1/2 teaspoon black pepper
- 6 bacon slices, cut in half
- ½ Cup mayonnaise
- 2 teaspoons of creamy wasabi (optional)
- 6 (1 oz.) sliced sharp cheddar cheese, cut in half (optional)
- Sliced red onion
- ½ Cup sliced kosher dill pickles
- 12 mini breads sliced horizontally
- Ketchup

Directions:

1. Place ground beef, garlic salt, seasoned salt, garlic powder, onion powder and black hupe pepper in a medium bowl.
2. Divide the meat mixture into 12 equal parts, shape into small thin round patties (about 2 ounces each) and save.

3. Cook the bacon on medium heat over medium heat for 5-8 minutes until crunchy. Set aside.

4. To make the sauce, mix the mayonnaise and horseradish in a small bowl, if used.

5. Set up a wood pellet smoker grill for direct cooking to use griddle accessories. Contact the manufacturer to see if there is a griddle accessory that works with the wooden pellet smoker grill.

6. Spray a cooking spray on the griddle cooking surface for best non-stick results.

7. Preheat wood pellet smoker grill to 350 °F using selected pellets. Griddle surface should be approximately 400 °F.

8. Grill the putty for 3-4 minutes each until the internal temperature reaches 160 °F.

9. If necessary, place a sharp cheddar cheese slice on each patty while the patty is on the griddle or after the patty is removed from the griddle. Place a small amount of mayonnaise mixture, a slice of red onion, and a hamburger pate in the lower half of each roll. Pickled slices, bacon, and ketchup.

36. **Garlic Parmesan Wedge**

Preparation Time: 15 minutes

Cooking Time: 30-35 minutes

Servings: 3

Recommended pellet: Optional

- 3 large russet potatoes
- ¼ cup of extra virgin olive oil
- 1 tsp salt
- ¾ teaspoon black hu pepper
- 2 tsp garlic powder
- ¾ cup grated parmesan cheese
- 3 tablespoons of fresh coriander or flat leaf parsley (optional)
- ½ cup blue cheese or ranch dressing per serving, for soaking (optional)

Directions:

1. Gently rub the potatoes with cold water using a vegetable brush to dry the potatoes.
2. Cut the potatoes in half vertically and cut them in half.
3. Wipe off any water released when cutting potatoes with a paper towel. Moisture prevents wedges from becoming crunchy.
4. Put the potato wedge, olive oil, salt, pepper, and garlic powder in a large bowl and shake lightly by hand to distribute the oil and spices evenly.
5. Place the wedges on a single layer of non-stick grill tray / pan / basket (about 15 x 12 inches).

6. Set the wood pellet r grill for indirect cooking and use all types of wood pellets to preheat to 425 degrees Fahrenheit.

7. Put the grill tray in the preheated smoker grill, roast the potato wedge for 15 minutes, and turn. Roast the potato wedge for an additional 15-20 minutes until the potatoes are soft inside and crispy golden on the outside.

8. Sprinkle potato wedge with parmesan cheese and add coriander or parsley as needed. If necessary, add blue cheese or ranch dressing for the dip.

37. Grilled Mushroom Skewers

Preparation Time: 5 Minutes

Cooking Time: 60 Minutes

Servings: 6

Ingredients:

- 16 - oz. 1 lb. Baby Portobello Mushrooms

For the marinade:

- ¼ - cup olive oil
- ¼ - cup lemon juice
- Small handful of parsley
- 1 - tsp sugar
- 1 - tsp salt
- ¼ - tsp pepper

- ¼ - tsp cayenne pepper
- 1 to 2 - garlic cloves
- 1 - Tbsp. balsamic vinegar

What you will need:

- 10 - inch bamboo/wood skewers

Directions:

1. Add the beans to the plate of a lipped container, in an even layer. Shower the softened spread uniformly out ludicrous, and utilizing a couple of tongs tenderly hurl the beans with the margarine until all around covered.

2. Season the beans uniformly, and generously, with salt and pepper.

3. Preheat the smoker to 275 degrees. Include the beans, and smoke 3-4 hours, hurling them like clockwork or until delicate wilted, and marginally seared in spots.

4. Spot 10 medium sticks into a heating dish and spread with water. It's critical to douse the sticks for in any event 15 minutes (more is better) or they will consume too rapidly on the flame broil.

5. Spot the majority of the marinade fixings in a nourishment processor and heartbeat a few times until marinade is almost smooth.

6. Flush your mushrooms and pat dry. Cut each mushroom down the middle, so each piece has half of the mushroom stem.

7. Spot the mushroom parts into an enormous gallon-size Ziploc sack, or a medium bowl and pour in the marinade. Shake the pack until the majority of the mushrooms are equally covered in marinade. Refrigerate and marinate for 30mins to 45mins.

8. Preheat your barbecue about 300F

9. Stick the mushrooms cozily onto the bamboo/wooden sticks that have been dousing (no compelling reason to dry the sticks). Piercing the mushrooms was a bit of irritating from the outset until I got the hang of things.

10. I've discovered that it's least demanding to stick them by bending them onto the stick. In the event that you simply drive the stick through, it might make the mushroom break.

11. Spot the pierced mushrooms on the hot barbecue for around 3mins for every side, causing sure the mushrooms don't consume to the flame broil. The mushrooms are done when they are delicate; as mushrooms ought to be Remove from the barbecue. Spread with foil to keep them warm until prepared to serve

Nutrition: Calories: 230 Carbs: 10g Fat: 20g Protein: 5g

38. Caprese Tomato Salad

Preparation Time: 5 Minutes

Cooking Time: 60 Minutes

Servings: 4

Ingredients:

- 3 - cups halved multicolored cherry tomatoes
- 1/8 - teaspoon kosher salt
- ½ - cup fresh basil leaves
- 1 - tablespoon extra-virgin olive oil
- 1 - tablespoon balsamic vinegar
- ½ - teaspoon black pepper
- ¼ - teaspoon kosher salt
- 1 - ounce diced fresh mozzarella cheese (about 1/3 cup)

Directions:

1. Join tomatoes and 1/8 tsp. legitimate salt in an enormous bowl. Let represent 5mins. Include basil leaves, olive oil, balsamic vinegar, pepper, 1/4 tsp. fit salt, and mozzarella; toss.

Nutrition: Calories 80 Fat 5.8g Protein 2g Carb 5g Sugars 4g

39. Watermelon-Cucumber Salad

Preparation Time: 12 Minutes

Cooking Time: 0 Minutes

Servings: 4

Ingredients:

- 1 - tablespoon olive oil
- 2 - teaspoons fresh lemon juice
- ¼ - teaspoon salt
- 2 - cups cubed seedless watermelon
- 1 - cup thinly sliced English cucumber
- ¼ - cup thinly vertically sliced red onion
- 1 - tablespoon thinly sliced fresh basil

Directions:

1. Consolidate oil, squeeze, and salt in a huge bowl, mixing great. Include watermelon, cucumber, and onion; toss well to coat. Sprinkle plate of mixed greens equally with basil.

Nutrition: Calories 60 Fat 3.5g Protein 0.8g Carb 7.6g

40. Fresh Creamed Corn

Preparation Time: 5 Minutes

Cooking Time: 30 Minutes

Servings: 4

Ingredients:

- 2 - teaspoons unsalted butter
- 2 - cups fresh corn kernels

- 2 - tablespoons minced shallots
- ¾ - cup 1% low-fat milk
- 2 - teaspoons all-purpose flour
- ¼ - teaspoon salt

Directions:
1. Melt butter in a huge nonstick skillet over medium-excessive warmness.
2. Add corn and minced shallots to pan; prepare dinner 1 minute, stirring constantly.
3. Add milk, flour, and salt to pan; bring to a boil.
4. Reduce warmness to low; cover and cook dinner 4 minutes.

Nutrition: Calories 107 Fat 3.4g Protein 4g Carb 18g

DINNER

41. Spinach Salad with Avocado and Orange

Preparation Time: 5 Minutes

Cooking Time: 20 Minutes

Servings: 4

Ingredients:

- 1 ½ - tablespoons fresh lime juice
- 4 - teaspoons extra-virgin olive oil
- 1 - tablespoon chopped fresh cilantro
- 1/8 - teaspoon kosher salt
- ½ - cup diced peeled ripe avocado
- ½ - cup fresh orange segments
- 1 - (5-ounce) package baby spinach
- 1/8 - teaspoon freshly ground black pepper

Directions:

1. Combine first 4 substances in a bowl, stirring with a whisk.
2. Combine avocado, orange segments, and spinach in a bowl. Add oil combination; toss. Sprinkle salad with black pepper.

Nutrition: Calories 103 Fat 7.3g Sodium 118mg

42. Raspberry and Blue Cheese Salad

Preparation Time: 5 Minutes

Cooking Time: 20 Minutes

Servings: 4

Ingredients:

- 1 ½ - tablespoons olive oil
- 1 ½ - teaspoons red wine vinegar
- ¼ - teaspoon Dijon mustard
- 1/8 - teaspoon salt
- 1/8 - teaspoon pepper
- 5 - cups mixed baby greens
- ½ - cup raspberries
- ¼ - cup chopped toasted pecans
- 1 - ounce blue cheese

Directions:

1. Join olive oil, vinegar, Dijon mustard, salt, and pepper.
2. Include blended infant greens; too.
3. Top with raspberries, walnuts, and blue cheddar.

Nutrition: Calories 133 Fat 12.2g Sodium 193mg

43. Crunchy Zucchini Chips

Preparation Time: 15 Minutes

Cooking Time: 25 Minutes

Servings: 4

Ingredients:

- 1/3 - cup whole-wheat panko
- 3 - tablespoons uncooked amaranth
- ½ - teaspoon garlic powder
- ¼ - teaspoon kosher salt
- ¼ - teaspoon freshly ground black pepper
- 1 - ounce Parmesan cheese, finely grated
- 12 - ounces zucchini, cut into
- ¼ - inch-thick slices
- 1 - tablespoon olive oil Cooking spray

Directions:

1. Preheat stove to 425°. Join the initial 6 ingre-dients in a shallow dish. Join zucchini and oil in an enormous bowl; toss well to coat. Dig zucchini in panko blend, squeezing tenderly to follow. Spot covered cuts on an ovenproof wire rack covered with cooking shower; place the rack on a preparing sheet or jam move dish.
2. Heat at 425° for 26 minutes or until cooked and fresh. Serve chips right away.

Nutrition: Calories 132 Fat 6.5g Protein 6g Carb 14g Sugars 2g

44. Grilled Green Onions and Orzo and Sweet Peas

Preparation Time: 5 Minutes

Cooking Time: 15 Minutes

Servings: 4

Ingredients:

- ¾ - cup whole-wheat orzo
- 1 - cup frozen peas
- 1 - bunch green onions, trimmed
- 1 - teaspoon olive oil
- ½ - teaspoon grated lemon rind
- 1 - tablespoon lemon juice
- 1 - teaspoon olive oil
- ¼ - teaspoon salt
- 1 - ounce shaved Montego cheese

Directions:

1. Plan orzo as indicated by way of headings, discarding salt and fat. Include peas throughout most recent 2mins of cooking; channel.
2. Warm a fish fry skillet over high warmness. Toss inexperienced onions with 1 teaspoon olive oil. Cook 2

minutes on each facet. Cleave onions; upload to orzo. Include lemon skin, lemon juice, 1 teaspoon olive oil, and salt; toss. Sprinkle with shaved Manchego cheddar.

Nutrition: Calories 197 Fat 5.6g Sodium 204mg

45. **Tequila Slaw with Lime and Cilantro**

Preparation Time: 5 Minutes

Cooking Time: 5 Minutes

Servings: 6

Ingredients:

- ¼ - cup canola mayonnaise (such as Hellmann's)
- 3 - tablespoons fresh lime juice
- 1 - tablespoon silver tequila
- 2 - teaspoons sugar
- ¼ - teaspoon kosher salt
- 1/3 - cup thinly sliced green onions
- ¼- cup chopped fresh cilantro
- 1 - (14-ounce) package coleslaw

Directions:

1. Add the first 5 ingredients in a big bowl. Add remaining ingredients; toss.

Nutrition: Calories 64 Fat 3g Protein 0.8g Carb 6.4g

46. Cranberry-Almond Broccoli Salad

Preparation Time: 10 Minutes

Cooking Time: 60 Minutes

Servings: 8

Ingredients:

- ¼ - cup finely chopped red onion
- 1/3 - cup canola mayonnaise
- 3 - tablespoons 2% reduced-fat Greek yogurt
- 1 - tablespoon cider vinegar
- 1 - tablespoon honey
- ¼ - teaspoon salt
- ¼ - teaspoon freshly ground black pepper
- 4 - cups coarsely chopped broccoli florets
- 1/3 - cup slivered almonds, toasted
- 1/3 - cup reduced-sugar dried cranberries
- 4 - center-cut bacon slices, cooked and crumbled

Directions:

1. Absorb red onion cold water for 5 minutes; channel.
2. Consolidate mayonnaise and then 5 fixings (through pepper), blending admirably with a whisk. Mix in red onion, broccoli, and remaining fixings. Spread and chill 1 hour before serving.

Nutrition: Calories 104 Fat 5.9g Carb 11g Sugars 5g

47. Grilled French Dip

Preparation Time: 15 Minutes

Cooking Time: 35 Minutes

Servings: 8 to 12

Ingredients:

- 3 lbs. onions, thinly sliced (yellow)
- 2 tbsp. oil
- 2 tbsp. of Butter
- Salt to taste
- Black pepper to taste
- 1 tsp. Thyme, chopped
- 2 tsp. of Lemon juice
- 1 cup Mayo
- 1 cup of Sour cream

Directions:

1. Preheat the grill to high with closed lid.
2. In a pan combine the oil and butter. Place on the grill to melt. Add 2 tsp. salt and add the onions.
3. Stir well and close the lid of the grill. Cook 30 minutes stirring often.

4. Add the thyme. Cook for an additional 3 minutes. Set aside and add black pepper.
5. Once cooled add lemon juice, mayo, and sour cream. Stir to combine.
6. Serve with veggies or chips. Enjoy!

Nutrition: Calories: 60 Protein: 4g Carbs: 5g Fat: 6g

48. Roasted Cashews

Preparation Time: 15 Minutes

Cooking Time: 12 Minutes

Servings: 6

Ingredients:

- ¼ cup Rosemary, chopped
- 2 ½ tbsp. Butter, melted
- 2 cups Cashews, raw
- ½ tsp. of Cayenne pepper
- 1 tsp. of salt

Directions:

1. Preheat the grill to 350F with closed lid.
2. In a baking dish layer, the nuts. Combine the cayenne, salt rosemary, and butter. Add on top.
3. Grill for 12 minutes.
4. Serve and enjoy!

Nutrition: Calories: 150 Proteins: 5g Carbs: 7g Fat: 15g

49. Smoked Jerky

Preparation Time: 20 Minutes

Cooking Time: 6 Hours

Servings: 6 to 8

Ingredients:

- 1 Flank Steak (3lb.)
- ½ cup of Brown Sugar
- 1 cup of Bourbon
- ¼ cup Jerky rub
- 2 tbsp. of Worcestershire sauce
- 1 can of Chipotle
- ½ cup Cider Vinegar

Directions:

1. Slice the steak into ¼ inch slices.
2. Combine the remaining ingredients in a bowl. Stir well.
3. Place the steak in a plastic bag and add the marinade sauce. Marinade in the fridge overnight.
4. Preheat the grill to 180F with closed lid.
5. Remove the flank from marinade. Place directly on a rack and on the grill.
6. Smoke for 6 hours.

7. Cover them lightly for 1 hour before serving. Store leftovers in the fridge.

Nutrition: Calories: 105 Protein: 14g Carbs 4g: Fat: 3g

50. **Bacon BBQ Bites**

Preparation Time: 10 Minutes

Cooking Time: 25 Minutes

Servings: 2 to 4

Ingredients:

- 1 tbsp. Fennel, ground
- ½ cup of Brown Sugar
- 1 lb. Slab Bacon, cut into cubes (1 inch)
- 1 tsp. Black pepper
- Salt

Directions:

1. Take an aluminum foil and then fold in half.
2. Preheat the grill to 350F with closed lid.
3. In a bowl combine the black pepper, salt, fennel, and sugar. Stir.
4. Place the pork in the seasoning mixture. Toss to coat. Transfer on the foil.
5. Place the foil on the grill. Bake for 25 minutes, or until crispy and bubbly.

6. Serve and enjoy!

Nutrition: Calories: 300 Protein: 27g Carbs: 4g Fat: 36g

51. **Smoked Guacamole**

Preparation Time: 25 Minutes

Cooking Time: 30 Minutes

Servings: 6 to 8

Ingredients:

- ¼ cup chopped Cilantro
- 7 Avocados, peeled and seeded
- ¼ cup chopped Onion, red
- ¼ cup chopped tomato
- 3 ears corn
- 1 tsp. of Chile Powder
- 1 tsp. of Cumin
- 2 tbsp. of Lime juice
- 1 tbsp. minced Garlic
- 1 Chile, poblano
- Black pepper and salt to taste

Directions:

1. Preheat the grill to 180F with closed lid.
2. Smoke the avocado for 10 min.

3. Set the avocados aside and increase the temperature of the girl to high.
4. Once heated grill the corn and chili. Roast for 20 minutes.
5. Cut the corn. Set aside. Place the chili in a bowl.
6. In a bowl mash the avocados, leave few chunks. Add the remaining ingredients and mix.
7. Serve right away because it is best eaten fresh. Enjoy!

Nutrition: Calories: 51 Protein: 1g Carbs: 3g Fat: 4.5g

52. Jalapeno Poppers

Preparation Time: 15 Minutes

Cooking Time: 60 Minutes

Servings: 4 to 6

Ingredients:

- 6 Bacon slices halved
- 12 Jalapenos, medium
- 1 cup grated Cheese
- 8 oz. softened Cream cheese
- 2 tbsp. Poultry seasoning

Directions:

1. Preheat the grill to 180F with closed lid.

2. Cut the jalapenos lengthwise. Clean them from the ribs and seeds.

3. Mix the poultry seasoning, grated cheese, and cream cheese.

4. Fill each jalapeno with the mixture and wrap with 1 half bacon. Place a toothpick to secure it.

5. Increase the temperature of the grill to 375F. Cook for 30 minutes more.

6. Serve and enjoy!

Nutrition: Calories: 60 Protein: 4g Carbs: 2g Fat: 8g

53. Shrimp Cocktail

Preparation Time: 10 Minutes

Cooking Time: 10 Minutes

Servings: 2 to 4

Ingredients:

- 2 lbs. of Shrimp with tails, deveined
- Black pepper and salt
- 1 tsp. of Old Bay
- 2 tbsp. Oil
- ½ cup of Ketchup
- 1 tbsp. of Lemon Juice
- 2 tbsp. Horseradish, Prepared

- 1 tbsp. of Lemon juice
- For garnish: chopped parsley
- Optional: Hot sauce

Directions:
1. Preheat the grill to 350F with closed lid.
2. Clean the shrimp. Pat dry using paper towels.
3. In a bowl add the shrimp, Old Bay, and oil. Toss to coat. Spread on a baking tray.
4. In the meantime, make the sauce: Combine the lemon juice, horseradish, and ketchup.
5. Serve the shrimp with the sauce and enjoy!

Nutrition: Calories: 80 Protein: 8g Carbs: 5g Fat: 1g

54. **Deviled Eggs**

Preparation Time: 15 Minutes

Cooking Time: 30 Minutes

Servings: 4 to 6

Ingredients:
- 3 tsp. diced chives
- 3 tbsp. Mayo
- 7 Eggs, hard - boiled, peeled
- 1 tsp. Cider vinegar
- 1 tsp. Mustard, brown

- 1/8 tsp. Hot sauce
- 2 tbsp. crumbled Bacon
- Black pepper and salt to taste
- For dusting: Paprika

Directions:

1. Preheat the grill to 180F with closed lid.
2. Place the cooked eggs on the grate. Smoke 30 minutes. Set aside and let them cool.
3. Slice the eggs in half lengthwise. Scoop the yolks and transfer into a Ziplock bag.
4. Cut one corner and squeeze the mixture into the egg whites.
5. Top with bacon and dust with paprika.
6. Serve and enjoy! Or chill in the fridge until serving.

Nutrition: Calories: 140 Protein: 6g Carbs: 2g Fat: 6g

55. **Smoked Summer Sausage**

Preparation Time: 15 Minutes

Cooking Time: 4 Hours

Servings: 4 to 6

Ingredients:

- 1 ½ tsp. of Morton Salt
- ½ lb. Ground venison

- ½ lb. of ground Boar
- 1 tbsp. Salt
- ½ tsp. of mustard seeds
- ½ tsp. of Garlic powder
- ½ tsp. of Black pepper

Directions:

1. Add all ingredients into a bowl and mix until combined. Cover the bowl with a plastic bag and let it rest in the fridge overnight
2. Form a log from the mixture and wrap with a plastic wrap. Twist the log's end tightly.
3. Preheat the grill to 225F with closed lit.
4. Grill the meat for 4 hours. Set aside and let it cool for 1 hour.
5. Once cooled wrap and store in the fridge.
6. Serve and enjoy!

Nutrition: Calories: 170 Protein: 8g Carbs: 0 Fat: 14g

56. Roasted Tomatoes

Preparation Time: 10 Minutes

Cooking Time: 3 Hours

Servings: 2 to 4

Ingredients:

- 3 ripe Tomatoes, large
- 1 tbsp. black pepper
- 2 tbsp. Salt
- 2 tsp. Basil
- 2 tsp. of Sugar
- Oil

Directions:

1. Place a parchment paper on a baking sheet. Preheat the grill to 225F with closed lid.
2. Remove the stems from the tomatoes. Cut them into slices (1/2 inch).
3. In a bowl combine the basil, sugar, pepper, and salt. Mix well.
4. Pour oil on a plate. Dip the tomatoes (just one side) in the oil.
5. Dust each slice with the mixture.
6. Grill the tomatoes for 3 hours.
7. Serve and enjoy! (You can serve it with mozzarella pieces).

Nutrition: Calories: 40 Protein: 1g Carbs: 2g Fat: 3g

57. **Onion Bacon Ring**

Preparation Time: 10 Minutes

Cooking Time: 1 Hour and 30 Minutes

Servings: 6 to 8

Ingredients:

- 2 large Onions, cut into ½ inch slices
- 1 Package of Bacon
- 1 tsp. of Honey
- 1 tbsp. Mustard, yellow
- 1 tbsp. Garlic chili sauce

Direction:

1. Wrap Bacon around onion rings. Wrap until you out of bacon. Place on skewers.
2. Preheat the grill to 400F with closed lid.
3. In the meantime, on a bowl combine the mustard and garlic chili sauce. Add honey and stir well.
4. Grill the onion bacon rings for 1 h and 30 minutes. Flip once.
5. Serve with the sauce and enjoy!

Nutrition: Calories: 90 Protein: 2g Carbs: 9g Fat: 7g

58. Grilled Watermelon

Preparation Time: 10 Minutes

Cooking Time: 15 Minutes

Servings: 4

Ingredients:

- 2 Limes
- 2 tbsp. oil
- ½ Watermelon, sliced into wedges
- ¼ Tsp. Pepper flakes
- 2 tbsp. Salt

Directions:

1. Preheat the grill to high with closed lid.
2. Brush the watermelon with oil. Grill for 15 minutes. Flip once.
3. In a blender mix the salt and pepper flakes until combined.
4. Transfer the watermelon on a plate.
5. Serve and enjoy!

Nutrition: Calories: 40 Protein: 1g Carbs: 10g Fat: 0

59. Smoked Popcorn with Parmesan Herb

Preparation Time: 10 Minutes

Cooking Time: 10 Minutes

Servings: 2 to 4

Ingredients:

- ¼ cup of Popcorn Kernels
- 1 tsp. of salt

- 1 tsp. of Garlic powder
- ½ cup grated Parmesan
- 2 tsp. of Italian seasoning
- 2 tbsp. oil
- 4 tbsp. of Butter

Directions:

1. Preheat the grill to 250F with closed lid.
2. In a saucepan add the butter and oil. Melt and add the salt, garlic powder, and Italian seasoning.
3. Add the kernels in a paper bag. Fold it two times to close.
4. Place in the microwave. Turn on high heat and set 2 minutes.
5. Open and transfer into a bowl.
6. Pour the butter. Toss. Transfer on a baking tray and grill for about 10 minutes.
7. Serve and enjoy!

Nutrition: Calories: 60 Protein: 1g Carbs: 5g Fat: 3g

60. Breakfast Sausage

Preparation Time: 60 minutes

Cooking Time: 9 hours

Servings: 6

Ingredients:

- 20/22-millimeter natural sheep casings, rinsed
- Warm water
- 2 lb. ground pork
- Apple butter rub
- Pinch dried marjoram
- 1/2 teaspoon ground cloves
- 1 tablespoon brown sugar
- 1/3 cup ice water
- Pepper to taste

Directions:

1. Soak the sheep casings in warm water for 1 hour.
2. In a bowl, mix all the ingredients.

3. Use a mixer set on low speed to combine the ingredients.
4. Cover and refrigerate the mixture for 15 minutes.
5. Insert the casings into the sausage stuffer.
6. Stuff the casings with the ground pork mixture.
7. Twist into five links.
8. Remove bubbles using a picker.
9. Put the sausages on a baking pan.
10. Refrigerate for 24 hours.
11. Set your wood pellet grill to smoke.
12. Hang the sausages on hooks and put them in the smoking cabinet.
13. Set the temperature to 350 degrees F.
14. Smoke the sausages for 1 hour.
15. Increase the temperature to 425 degrees F.
16. Cook for another 30 minutes.

Nutrition: Calories: 220 Fat: 19 g Cholesterol: 45 mg Carbohydrates: 1 g Fiber: 0 g Sugars: 1 g Protein: 11 g

61. **Corned Beef Hash**

Preparation Time: 30 minutes

Cooking Time: 4 hours

Servings: 4

Ingredients:
- 2 lb. corned beef brisket
- Pepper to taste
- 2 cups chicken broth
- 1 lb. potatoes, peeled
- 6 slices bacon, chopped
- 1 red bell pepper, chopped
- 1 onion, chopped
- 1 teaspoon thyme, chopped
- 1-1/2 teaspoon hickory bacon rub
- 2 tablespoons parsley, chopped

Directions:
1. Season the corned beef with the seasoning packet from its package and with the pepper.
2. Let it rest for 30 minutes.
3. Set your wood pellet grill to smoke for 10 to 15 minutes.
4. Set it to 225 degrees F.
5. Place the corned beef on top of the grills.
6. Smoke for 3 hours.
7. Transfer the corned beef to a baking pan.
8. Add the chicken broth and potatoes to the pan.
9. Cover the pan with foil.
10. Cook for 30 minutes.

11. Let the corned beef and potatoes cool.
12. Refrigerate for 1 hour.
13. Slice the potatoes and corned beef.
14. Add a cast-iron pan to the pellet grill.
15. Preheat it to 400 degrees F.
16. Cook the bacon until golden and crispy.
17. Transfer to a plate lined with a paper towel.
18. Add the red bell pepper and onion to the pan.
19. Cook for 3 minutes.
20. Stir in the corned beef.
21. Add the rest of the ingredients.
22. Serve while hot.

Nutrition: Calories: 380 Fat: 24 g Cholesterol: 80mg Carbohydrates: 22.1 g Fiber: 1.9 g Sugars: 1.1 g Protein: 20

62. Turkey Sandwich

Preparation Time: 10 minutes

Cooking Time: 20 minutes

Servings: 4

Ingredients:

- 8 bread slices
- 1 cup gravy
- 2 cups turkey, cooked and shredded

Directions:

1. Set your wood pellet grill to smoke.

2. Preheat it to 400 degrees F.
3. Place a grill mat on top of the grates.
4. Add the turkey on top of the mat.
5. Cook for 10 minutes.
6. Toast the bread in the flame broiler.
7. Top the bread with the gravy and shredded turkey.

Nutrition: Calories: 280 Fat: 3.5 g Cholesterol: 20 mg Carbohydrates: 46 g Fiber: 5 g Sugars: 7 g Protein: 18 g

63. Scrambled Eggs

Preparation Time: 5 Minutes

Cooking Time: 10 Minutes

Servings: 3 to 4

Ingredients:

- 1/4 cup Cheddar and Monterey Cheese Blend, shredded
- Sea Salt and Black Pepper, as needed
- 1 tbsp. Butter
- 6 Eggs
- 3 tbsp. Nut Milk or milk of your choice
- Green onion or fresh herbs of your choice, for garnish

Directions:

1. First, place eggs, milk, cheese blend, pepper, and salt in the blender pitcher.

2. Next, press the 'medium' button and blend the mixture for 25 to 30 seconds or until everything comes together and is frothy.
3. Then, heat the butter in a medium-sized saucepan over medium-low heat.
4. Once the skillet becomes hot and the butter has melted, swirl the pan so that the butter coats all the sides. Pour the egg mixture into it and allow it to sit for 20 seconds. With a spatula, break it down and continue cooking until the egg is set and cooked. Garnish with green onion. Serve it along with toasted bread.

Nutrition: Calories: 70 Fat: 5.6 g Total Carbs: 0.3 g Fiber: 0 g Sugar: 0.3 g Protein: 4.7 g Cholesterol: 157.5 mg

64. <u>Berry Smoothie</u>

Preparation Time: 5 Minutes

Cooking Time: 1 Minute

Servings: 1

Ingredients:

- 2 scoops Protein Powder
- 2 cups Almond Milk
- 4 cups Mixed Berry
- 2 cups Yoghurt

Directions:

1. First, place mixed berry, protein powder, yogurt, and almond milk in the blender pitcher. Then, select the 'smoothie' button. Finally, pour the smoothie into the serving glass.

Nutrition: Calories: 112 Fat: 2 g Total Carbs: 26 g Fiber: 0 g Sugar: 0 g Protein: 1 g Cholesterol: 0

APPETIZER AND SIDES

65. Avocado Smoothie

Preparation Time: 5 Minutes

Cooking Time: 5 Minutes

Servings: 2

Ingredients:

- 1 cup Coconut Milk, preferably full-fat
- 1 cup Ice
- 3 cups Baby Spinach
- 1 Banana, frozen and quartered
- 1/2 cup pineapple chunks, frozen
- 1/2 of 1 Avocado, smooth

Directions:

1. First, place ice, pineapple chunks, pineapple chunks, banana, avocado, baby spinach in the blender pitcher.

2. Now, press the 'extract' button.
3. Finally, transfer to a serving glass.

Nutrition: Fat: 25.1 g Calories: 323 Total Carbs: 29.2 g Fiber: 11.4 g Sugar: 8.3 g Protein: 5.1 g Cholesterol: 0

66. Tofu Smoothie

Preparation Time: 5 Minutes

Cooking Time: 5 Minutes

Servings: 2

Ingredients:

- 1 Banana, sliced and frozen
- 3/4 cup Almond Milk
- 2 tbsp. Peanut Butter
- 1/2 cup Yoghurt, plain and low-fat
- 1/2 cup Tofu, soft and silken
- 1/3 cup Dates, chopped

Directions:

1. First, place tofu, banana, dates, yogurt, peanut butter, and almond milk in the blender pitcher.
2. After that, press the 'smoothie' button.
3. Finally, transfer to the serving glass and enjoy it.

Nutrition: Fat: 0 g Calories: 330 Total Carbs: 0 g Fiber: 0 g Sugar: 0 g Protein: 0 g Cholesterol: 0

67. Banana Nut Oatmeal

Preparation Time: 5 Minutes

Cooking Time: 5 Minutes

Servings: 2

Ingredients:

- 1/2 tbsp. Maple Syrup
- 1/4 cup Hemp Seeds
- 1/2 cup Steel Cut Oats
- Dash of Sea Salt
- 1 tsp. Vanilla Extract
- 1/2 cup Water
- 1/2 tsp. Cinnamon
- 1 tsp. Nutmeg

- 1/3 cup Milk
- 1 Banana, medium, sliced and divided

Directions:

1. First, keep half of the banana, salt, oats, vanilla, cinnamon, almond milk, nutmeg, and maple syrup in the blender pitcher.
2. After that, press the 'cook' button and then the 'high' button.
3. Cook for 5 minutes.
4. Once done, divide the oatmeal among the serving bowls and top it with the remaining sliced banana and hemp seeds.

Nutrition: Fat: 5.3 g Calories: 189 Total Carbs: 34.9 g Fiber: 7.5 g Sugar: 15.3 g Protein: 3.9 g Cholesterol: 0

68. Carrot Strawberry Smoothie

Preparation Time: 5 Minutes

Cooking Time: 5 Minutes

Servings: 2

Ingredients:

- 1/3 cup Bell Pepper, diced
- 1 cup Carrot Juice, chilled
- 1 cup mango, diced
- 1 cup Strawberries, unsweetened and frozen

Directions:

1. To start with, place strawberries, bell pepper, and mango in the blender pitcher.
2. After that, pulse it a few times.
3. Next, pour the carrot juice into it.
4. Finally, press the 'smoothie' button.

Nutrition: Fat: 5.5 g Calories: 334 Total Carbs: 61 g Fiber: 12.7 g Sugar: 34 g Protein: 10.4 g Cholesterol: 7.5 mg

69. **Green Smoothie**

Preparation Time: 5 Minutes

Cooking Time: 5 Minutes

Servings: 3 to 4

Ingredients:

- 1/4 cup Baby Spinach
- 1/2 cup Ice
- 1/4 cup Kale
- 1/2 cup Pineapple Chunks
- 1/2 cup Coconut Water
- 1/2 cup mango, diced
- 1/2 banana, diced

Directions:

1. Begin by placing all the ingredients needed to make the smoothie in the blender pitcher.
2. Now, press the 'extract' button.
3. Transfer the smoothie into the serving glass.

Nutrition: Calories: 184 Fat: 1.3 g Total Carbs: 44.6 g Fiber: 4.5 g Sugar: 21.9 g Protein: 4.3 g Choleterol: 0

70. **Kid-friendly Zucchini Bread**

Preparation Time: 15 minutes

Cooking Time: 50 minutes

Servings: 4

Ingredients:

- 1 ½ cup whole wheat flour
- 2 eggs
- 1 tsp salt
- 1 tsp baking powder
- 1 tsp baking soda
- ½ cup maple syrup
- 4 tbsp butter (melted)
- 2 tsp cinnamon
- 2 tsp vanilla extract
- 1 ½ cups shredded zucchini
- 2 tbsp lemon juice
- 1 tsp ground nutmeg

Directions:

1. Start your grill on smoke mode, leave the lip open for 5 minutes, or until the fire starts.
2. Close the lid and preheat the grill to 350°F for 15 minutes, using apple hardwood pellets.
3. Wrap the shredded zucchini with a clean kitchen towel and squeeze to remove excess liquid. Set aside.
4. In a mixing bowl, whisk together the eggs, maple syrup, butter, vanilla extract, and lemon juice.
5. Pour the egg mixture into the flour mixture and mix until the ingredients are well combined.
6. Fold in the shredded zucchini.

7. Pour the batter into the prepared loaf pan and spread it to the edges of the pan.
8. Place the loaf pan directly on the grill and bake until a toothpick inserted in the middle of the bread comes out clean.
9. Remove the loaf pan from the grill and transfer the bread to a wire rack to cool.
10. Serve and enjoy.

Nutrition: Calories: 428 Total Fat: 14.6 g Saturated Fat: 8.3 g Cholesterol: 112 mg Sodium: 1020 mg Total Carbohydrate 66 g Dietary Fiber 2.5 g Total Sugars: 25.1 g Protein: 8.4 g

71. Breakfast Sausage Casserole

Preparation Time: 15 minutes

Cooking Time: 30 minutes

Servings: 6

Ingredients:

- 1-pound ground sausage
- 1 tsp ground sage
- ¼ cup green beans (chopped)
- 2 tsp yellow mustard
- 1 tsp cayenne
- 8 tbsp mayonnaise
- 1 large onion (diced)
- 2 cups diced zucchini
- 2 cups shredded cabbage

- 1 ½ cup shredded cheddar cheese
- Chopped fresh parsley to taste

Directions:
1. Preheat the grill to 360°F and grease a cast-iron casserole dish.
2. Heat a large skillet over medium to high heat.
3. Toss the sausage into the skillet, break it apart and cook until browned, stirring constantly.
4. Add the cabbage, zucchini, green beans, and onion and cook until the vegetables are tender, stirring frequently.
5. Pour the cooked sausage and vegetable into the casserole dish and spread it.
6. Break the eggs into a mixing bowl and add the mustard, cayenne, mayonnaise, and sage. Whish until well combined.
7. Stir in half of the cheddar cheese.
8. Pour the egg mixture over the ingredients in the casserole dish.
9. Sprinkle with the remaining shredded cheese.
10. Place the baking dish on the grill and bake until the top of the casserole turns golden brown.
11. Garnish with chopped fresh parsley.

Nutrition: Calories: 472 Total Fat: 37.6 g Saturated Fat: 13.9 g Cholesterol: 98 mg Sodium: 909 mg Total Carbohydrate 10.7 g Dietary Fiber 1.9 g Total Sugars: 4 g Protein: 23.1 g

72. Keto Quiche

Preparation Time: 10 minutes

Cooking Time: 45 minutes

Servings: 6

Ingredients:

- 12 tbsp unsalted butter (soften)
- 12 large eggs
- 8 ounces grated cheddar cheese (divided)
- 4 ounces cream cheese
- ½ tsp salt or to taste
- ½ tsp ground black pepper or to taste
- 1 yellow onion (diced)
- 1 green bell pepper (chopped)
- 3 cups broccoli florets (chopped)
- 1 tbsp olive oil

Directions:

1. Preheat the grill to 325°F with the lid closed for 15 minutes.

2. Heat the olive oil in a skillet over high heat.
3. Add the chopped onion, broccoli, and green pepper. Cook for about 8 minutes, stirring constantly.
4. Remove the skillet from heat.
5. Process the egg and cheese in a food processor, adding the melted butter in a bit while processing.
6. Combine 4ounce grated cheddar cheese, salt, and pepper in a quiche pan.
7. Toss the cooked vegetable into the pan and mix.
8. Pour the egg mixture over the ingredients in the quiche pan.
9. Sprinkle the remaining grated cheese over it.
10. Place the pan in the preheated grill and bake for 45 minutes.
11. Remove and transfer the quiche to a rack to cool.
12. Slice and serve.

Nutrition: Calories: 615 Total Fat: 54.7 g Saturated Fat: 30.1 g Cholesterol: 494 mg Sodium: 804 mg Total Carbohydrate 8.1 g Dietary Fiber 1.9 g Total Sugars: 3.6 g Protein: 25.4 g

73. **Smoked and Pulled Beef**

Preparation Time: 10 minutes

Cooking Time: 6 hours

Servings: 6

Ingredients:

- 4 lb. beef sirloin tip roast
- 1/2 cup BBQ rub
- 2 bottles of amber beer
- 1 bottle barbecues sauce

Directions:

1. Turn your wood pellet grill on smoke setting then trim excess fat from the steak.

2. Coat the steak with BBQ rub and let it smoke on the grill for 1 hour.
3. Continue cooking and flipping the steak for the next 3 hours. Transfer the steak to a braising vessel. Add the beers.
4. Braise the beef until tender then transfer to a platter reserving 2 cups of cooking liquid.
5. Use a pair of forks to shred the beef and return it to the pan. Add the reserved liquid and barbecue sauce. Stir well and keep warm before serving.
6. Enjoy.

Nutrition: Calories 829, Total fat 46g, Saturated fat 18g, Total carbs 4g, Net carbs 4g, Protein 86g, Sugar 0g, Fiber 0g, Sodium: 181mg

74. Wood Pellet Smoked Beef Jerky

Preparation Time: 15 minutes

Cooking Time: 5 hours

Servings: 10

Ingredients:

- 3 lb sirloin steaks, sliced into 1/4-inch thickness
- 2 cups soy sauce
- 1/2 cup brown sugar
- 1 cup pineapple juice
- 2 tbsp sriracha
- 2 tbsp red pepper flake
- 2 tbsp hoisin
- 2 tbsp onion powder
- 2 tbsp rice wine vinegar
- 2 tbsp garlic, minced

Directions:

1. Mix all the ingredients in a zip lock-bag. Seal the bag and mix until the beef is well coated. Ensure you get as much air as possible from the zip-lock bag.
2. Put the bag in the fridge overnight to let marinate. Remove the bag from the fridge 1 hour before cooking.
3. Start your wood pallet grill and set it to smoke. Layout the meat on the grill with half-inch space between them.
4. Let them cook for 5 hours while turning after every 2-1/2 hours.
5. Transfer from the grill and let cool for 30 minutes before serving.
6. enjoy.

Nutrition: Calories 80, Total fat 1g, Saturated fat 0g, Total carbs 5g, Net carbs 5g, Protein 14g, Sugar 5g,

Fiber 0g, Sodium: 650mg

75. **Reverse Seared Flank Steak**

Preparation Time: 10 minutes

Cooking Time: 10 minutes

Servings: 2

Ingredients:

- 1.5 lb Flanks steak
- 1 tbsp salt
- 1/2 onion powder
- 1/4 tbsp garlic powder
- 1/2 black pepper, coarsely ground

Directions:

1. Preheat your wood pellet grill to 225f
2. In a mixing bowl, mix salt, onion powder, garlic powder, and pepper. Generously rub the steak with the mixture.
3. Place the steaks on the preheated grill, close the lid, and let the steak cook.
4. Crank up the grill to high then let it heat. The steak should be off the grill and tented with foil to keep it warm.
5. Once the grill is heated up to 450°F, place the steak back and grill for 3 minutes per side.
6. Remove from heat, pat with butter, and serve. Enjoy.

Nutrition: Calories 112, Total fat 5g, Saturated fat 2g, Total carbs 1g, Net carbs 1g, Protein 16g, Sugar 0g, Fiber 0g, Sodium: 737mg

76. Smoked Midnight Brisket

Preparation Time: 15 minutes

Cooking Time: 12 hours

Servings: 6

Ingredients:

- 1 tbsp Worcestershire sauce
- 1 tbsp Traeger beef Rub
- 1 tbsp Traeger Chicken rub
- 1 tbsp Traeger Blackened Saskatchewan rub
- 5 lb. flat cut brisket
- 1 cup beef broth

Directions:

1. Rub the sauce and rubs in a mixing bowl then rub the mixture on the meat.
2. Preheat your grill to 180°F with the lid closed for 15 minutes. You can use super smoke if you desire.
3. Place the meat on the grill and grill for 6 hours or until the internal temperature reaches 160°F.
4. Remove the meat from the grill and double wrap it with foil.
5. Add beef broth and return to grill with the temperature increased to 225°F. Cook for 4 hours or until the internal temperature reaches 204°F.
6. Remove from the grill and let rest for 30 minutes. Serve and enjoy with your favorite BBQ sauce.

Nutrition: Calories 200, Total fat 14g, Saturated fat 6g, Total carbs 3g, Net carbs 3g, Protein 14g, Sugar 0g, Fiber 0g, Sodium: 680mg

77. Grilled Butter Basted Porterhouse Steak

Preparation Time: 10 minutes

Cooking Time: 40 minutes

Servings: 4

Ingredients:

- 4 tbsp butter, melted
- 2 tbsp Worcestershire sauce
- 2 tbsp Dijon mustard
- Traeger Prime rib rub

Directions:

1. Set your wood pellet grill to 225°F with the lid closed for 15 minutes.

2. In a mixing bowl, mix butter, sauce, Dijon mustard until smooth. brush the mixture on the meat then season with the rub.
3. Arrange the meat on the grill grate and cook for 30 minutes.
4. Use tongs to transfer the meat to a pattern then increase the heat to high.
5. Return the meat to the grill grate to grill until your desired doneness is achieved.
6. Baste with the butter mixture again if you desire and let rest for 3 minutes before serving. Enjoy.

Nutrition: Calories 726, Total fat 62g, Saturated fat 37g, Total carbs 5g, Net carbs 4g, Protein 36g, Sugar 1g, Fiber 1g, Sodium: 97mg, Potassium 608mg

78. Cocoa Crusted Grilled Flank steak

Preparation Time: 10 minutes

Cooking Time: 6 minutes

Servings: 6

Ingredients:

- 1 tbsp cocoa powder
- 2 tbsp chili powder
- 1 tbsp chipotle chili powder
- 1/2 tbsp garlic powder
- 1/2 tbsp onion powder
- 1-1/2 tbsp brown sugar

- 1 tbsp cumin
- 1 tbsp smoked paprika
- 1 tbsp kosher salt
- 1/2 tbsp black pepper
- Olive oil
- 4 lb. Flank steak

Directions:
1. Whisk together cocoa, chili powder, garlic powder, onion powder, sugar, cumin, paprika, salt, and pepper in a mixing bowl.
2. Drizzle the steak with oil then rub with the cocoa mixture on both sides.
3. Preheat your wood pellet grill for 15 minutes with the lid closed.
4. Cook the meat on the grill grate for 5 minutes or until the internal temperature reaches 135°F.
5. Remove the meat from the grill and let it cool for 15 minutes to allow the juices to redistribute.
6. Slice the meat against the grain and on a sharp diagonal.
7. Serve and enjoy.

Nutrition: Calories 420, Total fat 26g, Saturated fat 8g, Total carbs 21g, Net carbs 13g, Protein 3g, Sugar 7g, Fiber 8g, Sodium: 2410mg

79. **Wood Pellet Grill Prime Rib Roast**

Preparation Time: 10 minutes

Cooking Time: 4 hours

Servings: 10

Ingredients:

- 7 lb. bone prime rib roast
- Traeger prime rib rub

Directions:

1. Coat the roast generously with the rub then wrap in a plastic wrap. let sit in the fridge for 24 hours to marinate.
2. Set the temperatures to 500°F.to to preheat with the lid closed for 15 minutes.
3. Place the rib directly on the grill fat side up and cook for 30 minutes.
4. Reduce the temperature to 300°F and cook for 4 hours or until the internal temperature is 120°F-rare, 130°F-medium rare, 140°F-medium, and 150°F-well done.
5. Remove from the grill and let rest for 30 minutes then serve and enjoy.

Nutrition: Calories 290, Total fat 23g, Saturated fat 9.3g, Protein 19g, Sodium: 54mg, Potassium 275mg

80. Smoked Longhorn Cowboy Tri-Tip

Preparation Time: 10 minutes

Cooking Time: 4 hours

Servings: 7

Ingredients:

- 3 lb tri-tip roast 1/8 cup coffee, ground
- 1/4 cup Traeger beef rub

Directions:

1. Preheat the grill to 180°F with the lid closed for 15 minutes. Meanwhile, rub the roast with coffee and beef rub. Place the roast on the grill grate and smoke for 3 hours. Remove the roast from the grill and double wrap it with foil. Increase the temperature to 275°F. Return the meat to the grill and let cook for 90 minutes or until the internal temperature reaches 135°F.

2. Remove from the grill, unwrap it and let rest for 10 minutes before serving.

Nutrition: Calories 245, Total fat 14g, Saturated fat 4g, Protein 23g, Sodium: 80mg

81. <u>Wood Pellet Grill Teriyaki Beef Jerky</u>

Preparation Time: 10 minutes

Cooking Time: 5 hours

Servings: 6

Ingredients:

- 3 cups soy sauce
- 2 cups brown sugar
- 3 garlic cloves
- 2-inch ginger knob, peeled and chopped
- 1 tbsp sesame oil
- 4 lb. beef, skirt steak

Directions:

1. Place all the ingredients except the meat in a food processor. Pulse until well mixed.
2. Trim any excess fat from the meat and slice into 1/4-inch slices. Add the steak with the marinade into a zip lock bag and let marinate for 12-24 hours in a fridge.
3. Set the wood pellet grill to smoke and let preheat for 5 minutes.
4. Arrange the steaks on the grill leaving a space between each. Let smoke for 5 hours.
5. Remove the steak from the grill and serve when warm.

Nutrition: Calories 80, Total fat 1g, Saturated fat 0g, Total Carbs 7g, Net Carbs 0g, Protein 11g, Sugar 6g,

Fiber 0g, Sodium: 390mg

82. Grilled Butter Basted Rib-eye

Preparation Time: 20 minutes

Cooking Time: 25 minutes

Servings: 4

Ingredients:

- 2 rib-eye steaks, bone-in
- Salt to taste
- Pepper to taste
- 4 tbsp butter, unsalted

Directions:

1. Mix steak, salt, and pepper in a zip-lock bag. Seal the bag and mix until the beef is well coated. Ensure you get as much air as possible from the zip-lock bag.
2. Set the wood pellet grill temperature to high with the lid closed for 15 minutes. Place a cast-iron into the grill.
3. Place the steaks on the hottest spot of the grill and cook for 5 minutes with the lid closed.
4. Open the lid and add butter to the skillet. When it's almost melted place the steak on the skillet with the grilled side up.
5. Cook for 5 minutes while busting the meat with butter. Close the lid and cook until the internal temperature is 130°F.
6. Remove the steak from the skillet and let rest for 10 minutes before enjoying with the reserved butter.

Nutrition: Calories 745, Total fat 65g, Saturated fat 32g, Total Carbs 5g, Net Carbs 5g, Protein 35g,

83. **Wood Pellet Smoked Brisket**

Preparation Time: 20 minutes

Cooking Time: 9 hours

Servings: 10

Ingredients:

- 2 tbsp garlic powder
- 2 tbsp onion powder
- 2 tbsp paprika
- 2 tbsp chili powder
- 1/3 cup salt
- 1/3 cup black pepper
- 12 lb whole packer brisket, trimmed
- 1-1/2 cup beef broth

Directions:

1. Set your wood pellet temperature to 225°F. Let preheat for 15 minutes with the lid closed.
2. Meanwhile, mix garlic, onion, paprika, chili, salt, and pepper in a mixing bowl.
3. Season the brisket generously on all sides.

4. Place the meat on the grill with the fat side down and let it cool until the internal temperature reaches 160°F. Remove the meat from the grill and double wrap it with foil. Return it to the grill and cook until the internal temperature reaches 204°F.
5. Remove from the grill, unwrap the brisket, and let sit for 15 minutes.
6. Slice and serve.

Nutrition: Calories 270, Total fat 20g, Saturated fat 8g, Total Carbs 3g, Net Carbs 3g, Protein 20g, Sugar 1g, Fiber 0g, Sodium: 1220mg

84. Traeger Beef Jerky

Preparation Time: 15 minutes

Cooking Time: 5 hours

Servings: 10

Ingredients:

- 3 lb. sirloin steaks
- 2 cups soy sauce
- 1 cup pineapple juice

- 1/2 cup brown sugar
- 2 tbsp sriracha
- 2 tbsp hoisin
- 2 tbsp red pepper flake
- 2 tbsp rice wine vinegar
- 2 tbsp onion powder

Directions:

1. Mix the marinade in a zip lock bag and add the beef. Mix until well coated and remove as much air as possible.
2. Place the bag in a fridge and let marinate overnight or for 6 hours. Remove the bag from the fridge an hour before cooking 3) Startup the Traeger and set it on the smoking settings or at 1900F.
3. Lay the meat on the grill leaving a half-inch space between the pieces. Let cool for 5 hours and turn after 2 hours.
4. Remove from the grill and let cool. Serve or refrigerate

Nutrition: Calories 309, Total fat 7g, Saturated fat 3g, Total carbs 20g, Net carbs 19g Protein 34g, Sugars 15g,

Fiber 1g, Sodium 2832mg

85. Traeger Smoked Beef Roast

Preparation Time: 10 minutes

Cooking Time: 6 hours

Servings: 6

Ingredients:

- 1-3/4 lb. beef sirloin tip roast
- 1/2 cup BBQ rub
- 2 bottles of amber beer
- 1 bottle BBQ sauce

Directions:

1. Turn the Traeger onto the smoke setting.
2. Transfer the beef to a pan and add the beer. The beef should be 1/2 way covered.
3. Braise the beef until fork tender. It will take 3 hours on the stovetop and 60 minutes on the instant pot.
4. Remove the beef from the ban and reserve 1 cup of the cooking liquid.
5. Use 2 forks to shred the beef into small pieces then return to the pan with the reserved braising liquid.
6. Add BBQ sauce and stir well then keep warm until serving. You can also reheat if it gets cold.

Nutrition: Calories 829, Total fat 46g, Saturated fat 18g, Total carbs 4g, Net carbs 4g Protein 86g, Sugars 0g,

Fiber 0g, Sodium 181mmg

86. Reverse Seared Flank Steak

Preparation Time: 10 minutes

Cooking Time: 20 minutes

Servings: 2

Ingredients:

- 3 lb. flank steaks
- 1 tbsp salt
- 1/2 tbsp onion powder
- 1/4 tbsp garlic powder
- 1/2 black pepper, coarsely ground

Directions:

1. Preheat the Traeger to 2250F.
2. All the ingredients in a bowl and mix well. Add the steaks and rub them generously with the rub mixture. Place the steak on the grill and close the lid. Let cook until its internal temperature is 100F under your desired temperature. 1150F for rare, 1250F for the medium rear,

and 1350F for medium. Wrap the steak with foil and raise the grill temperature to high. Place back the steak and grill for 3 minutes on each side. Pat with butter and serve when hot.

Nutrition: Calories 112, Total fat 5g, Saturated fat 2g, Total carbs 1g, Net carbs 1g Protein 16g, Sodium 737mg

87. Traeger Beef Tenderloin

Preparation Time: 10 minutes

Cooking Time: 45 minutes

Servings: 6

Ingredients:

- 4 lb. beef tenderloin
- 3 tbsp steak rub
- 1 tbsp kosher salt

Directions:

1. Preheat the Traeger to high heat. Meanwhile, trim excess fat from the beef and cut it into 3 pieces. Coat the steak with rub and kosher salt. Place it on the grill.

Close the lid and cook for 10 minutes. Open the lid, flip the beef and cook for 10 more minutes. Reduce the temperature of the grill to 2250F and smoke the beef until the internal temperature reaches 1300F.
2. Remove the beef from the grill and let rest for 15 minutes before slicing and serving.

Nutrition: Calories 999, Total fat 76g, Saturated fat 30g, Protein 74g, Sodium 1234mmg

CONCLUSION

Other than things you need to know about Trager Grill, you must also need to learn things about your meats.

So, here are some tips when preparing your meat for grilling?

- Marinate the meat overnight for maximum flavor.
- Bring meat to room temperature before cooking so it cooks evenly.
- Cook over moderate heat in a pan or on a grill, turning occasionally.
- Try grilling with flavorful sauces or marinades such as teriyaki, barbecue sauce, or salsa Verde.

Next will be how to choose your meat that are perfect for grilling?

- Avoid the fat marbling.
- Choose the meat with the most surface area in contact with the grilling surface, in order to get maximum flavor and even cooking.
- Medium rare is preferable for beef steaks or roasts. For pork and chicken, cook until the thickest part of each piece registers 160°F on an instant-read thermometer.

These are things you need to know about your meat and how to choose them because it is related with how to choose your Trager grill for example the best charcoal grill and gas grill for you.

Speaking of that, next will be how to choose your pellet?

Trager uses pellets for this grill. Yes, we all know that pellets are made of compressed wood byproducts and it is also easy to use.

- Pellets are more consistent in the flavor and the heat than normal charcoal.
- Pellets can be burned hotter and cleaner, producing more smoke than ordinary charcoal briquettes and converting the smoke into highly flavorful vapor.

- If you want to see more advantages of pellets, you can find out because it has many advantages over other types of fuel for grilling meat such as wood chips or lump charcoal.

Another thing that is about choice is how to choose your best lighter fluid for Trager grill?

Lighter fluid is not necessarily needed on this grill. The best thing to do is to add charcoal and wood chips as well as add more side fire if needed, once the food has started to grill.

- Never breathe in the fumes of the lighter fluid.
- Keep it away from children and pets.
- Open windows or doors when applying them.
- Never store near or use them near an open flame, as this can cause the fluid to catch fire.
- Store in a cool, dry place away from heat and in a well labeled container out of the reach of children and pets.
- When you are done using it, close the cap tightly before throwing it out.

So far are things that you need to know about Trager grill and your meat so if you want to get better results for grilling with Trager grill, you should also follow these things before starting your cooking process.

 Congratulations! You have read and finished this book about how to choose your Trager grill that is perfect for you as well as how to choose your meat and your lighter fluid.

Thank you for your support and I wish you a happy and delightful grilling experience.

© 2021, Stephen Gilbert
Herstellung und Verlag: BoD – Books on Demand, Norderstedt
ISBN: 9783755714392